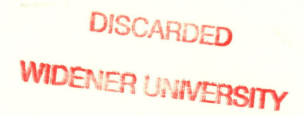

Emerging
Influentials
in
State
Legislatures

Emerging
Influentials
in
State
Legislatures

WOMEN, BLACKS, AND HISPANICS

Albert J. Nelson

New York
Westport, Connecticut
London

Library of Congress Cataloging-in-Publication Data

Nelson, Albert J.
  Emerging influentials in state legislatures : women, Blacks, and
Hispanics / Albert J. Nelson.
    p.   cm.
  Includes bibliographical references and index.
  ISBN 0-275-93829-8 (alk. paper)
    1. Legislative bodies—United States—States—Committees.
  2. Legislative bodies—United States—States—Leadership. 3. Women
  legislators—United States—States. 4. Afro-American legislators—
  United States—States. 5. Hispanic American legislators—United
  States—States. I. Title.
  JK2495.N45   1991
  328.73'076–dc20   91-8604

British Library Cataloguing in Publication Data is available.

Library of Congress Catalog Card Number: 91-8604
ISBN: 0-275-93829-8
First published in 1991

Praeger Publishers, One Madison Avenue, New York, NY 10010
An imprint of Greenwood Publishing Group, Inc.

Printed in the United States of America

The paper used in this book complies with the
Permanent Paper Standard issued by the National
Information Standards Organization (Z39.48–1984).

10   9   8   7   6   5   4   3   2   1

Dedicated to

My Family for Their Patience

CONTENTS

LIST OF TABLES

Emerging
Influentials
in
State
Legislatures

1

INTRODUCTION TO MINORITY INCORPORATION

In the past two decades, increased numbers of women, blacks, and Hispanics have been elected to state legislatures. Their numbers, especially in lower state legislative chambers, are increasing. But how much influence does this represent? Being there is important — a symbolic recognition that as a group they have arrived as important role models to the rest of the community, but their presence reveals little of their effective influence.[1] They need committee chairs and party leadership roles, and ideally these should be within each chamber's dominant party. Only then can they help determine legislative agendas and policies and thus gain benefits for their constituents, including members of their own minority. In this sense, they must not only gain entry, but they must also become fully incorporated into a legislature. They must "get into the club" to obtain "sustained influence and responsiveness" to group interests.[2]

For each of these minority groups, different factors are likely to affect representation, turnover, and potential influence — all part of the process of incorporation. I will use three rather artificial factors to explain incorporation within the legislatures: opportunity and incentives, party, and demographic characteristics. Do minorities, as other male Republican and Democratic representatives, seek political office because the salary is better or because there are leadership positions to make a mark in one's life? What is the impact on minority representation of multimember districts, other opportunity and incentives, local party organizations, traditional party organization states, and party control of legislatures? What impact do cultural values, cultural groups, and other traditional state characteristics have on participation? What are the effects of different elections (reapportionment, presidential, and off-year) on the process of incorporation in the 1980s?

EXPLAINING INCORPORATION

Getting elected, representing constituents in committees and party conferences, and staying in a legislative chamber long enough to fully develop one's influence represent the dynamic process of incorporation. Successful incorporation is important because state legislatures are a "breeding ground for political ambition" and further political mobility.[3] If legislative service is rewarding, a legislator is likely to remain in office. If an opportunity for higher office presents itself, a representative is likely to seize the propitious moment. If no opportunity presents itself, one may expect the satisfied legislator to remain in office and extend personal influence and effectiveness.

Opportunity and Incentives

One may expect that legislatures differ in terms of the opportunities and incentives provided legislators. Some legislators exist in environments conducive to political action and advancement. Other situations provide incentives for a state legislative career, or they may simply represent a "dead end" with few opportunities to advance or incentives to remain. Elder Witt can be said to agree with Peverill Squire that government leaders may not be paid enough to retain the interest of the most capable.[4] Legislative salaries could affect incorporation, that is, minority representation, turnover, and the potential influence of these groups (not to mention the quality of legislative professionalism). Irene Diamond and Wilma Rule found no relationship between legislative salaries and women's representation, but they did not differentiate between Democratic and Republican women, and this study adds blacks and Hispanics.[5]

Like legislative salaries, the number of possible leadership positions, especially committee chairs, may also have an important effect, and obtaining committee chairs can be affected by other legislative peers. Lower chamber leaders have great latitude in the appointment of members and officers to committees. Committee leadership is important because it suggests influence in centers of specialization.[6] When there is competition for a position, a more senior member is likely to obtain it, but generally the criterion for membership in committees is found in a member's background, experience, or ideological predispositions.[7] However, the leaders' latitude in the use of incentives can be quite important to new minorities entering the legislature. How will each be treated? Do the leaders stereotype and discriminate? Such treatment might affect minority stability and increase turnover. A decade ago women reported these fears and were concerned that they would not be able to move up the leadership hierarchy and make a real difference in policy making.[8]

The evidence is mixed. Research indicates that women and blacks have sensitized their white male counterparts to their interests. Logically, a similar experience may affect Hispanics as well, but, in any case, leaders can manipulate incentives that affect political ambition. In contemporary state legislatures, conflict is dysfunctional. Leaders, as Wayne Francis acknowledges, may use an "accommodation" approach to respond to a legislator's committee preferences.[9] Hence, one keeps members satisfied by providing legislative positions that meet leadership and membership expectations.

The legislature's specialized committee system provides each legislator ample opportunity to pursue several goals. Legislators may help constituents solve problems with the state bureaucracy through casework, make "good" policy that goes beyond pork barrel for constituents, or seek legislative posts to affect the policy agenda.[10] Mayhew might argue that the committee system is an appropriate arena where legislators may take credit for legislative action by generating beliefs that they are "personally responsible for causing government . . . to do something" desirable.[11] A major assumption of this research is that representatives will try to obtain legislative positions to pursue personal and constituent goals. Doing so is likely to be difficult because constituent policy preferences are not easy to gauge. Still, legislators do try to gauge constituent interests although their relative success is greater if the issue is strongly salient to district voters.[12]

We may predict that minorities would have memberships in committees concerned with policy issues reflecting symbolic and economic community needs. Symbolically, all three groups face stereotypes that have structured political opportunity.[13] Hence these groups seek public recognition of equal capacities whose development depends on equal opportunity. However, the equal opportunity found in civil rights statutes is not a sufficient protection of minority interests. How have they softened the feminization of poverty and the decline of services in the central cities, especially the educational system so crucial to equal opportunity? Economic policies associated with public and private decisions are a major concern, particularly for blacks and Hispanics who are represented in large segregated tracts of U.S. central cities. A serious social crisis in northern, southern, and southwestern cities has been further exacerbated by huge federal deficits that may make important policy shifts favorable to these groups more difficult to obtain.[14]

Perhaps black constituents among these minority groups are most stable and predictable on issues of civil rights, social welfare, and the issue of regressive taxation. Many of these same issues are likely to be critical to large urban Hispanic voting blocs as well, although a good part of their interest on education focuses on bilingual, bicultural issues.[15]

Women are expected to reflect the concerns and issues associated with cultural conditioning that structures their interests (women are likely to perform nurturing roles). This conditioning then determines the committees they are likely to dominate. Shayne Merritt reflects on women's sex roles and concludes that women are more "public-serving" than men who seem more "private-serving" in politics. By Merritt's definition, service on public-serving committees would include, for example, education and public welfare. Historically, women have been intellectual and political leaders in social welfare policy and, of course, policy concerned with civil liberties and the substantive economic issues facing women today.[16] A similar pattern of incorporation in committees is likely for blacks and Hispanics, who also face stereotypes in addition to the socioeconomic problems of their central city constituencies, and for some southern blacks with constituents in the rural South. With these issue interests in mind, the assessment of incorporation of these minority groups should provide important keys to their present and possible future political influence.

Minority opportunity may also be affected by the existence of multimember districts, changes in the size of chambers, and the likely competition for seats. If a state has a system of multimember district representation, it affects the representation of these minorities differently. Contemporary evidence indicates that women's representation is favored to the detriment of other minorities. Under certain conditions, multimember districts have been used to dilute a geographically compact urban racial minority that would otherwise constitute a majority in a single-member district plan. In addition, turnover is likely to be greater in these states.[17] However, do the effects of multimember district representation and turnover affect Republican and Democratic females equally, particularly those who are not black or Hispanic? Other regional or party factors could have varying degrees of influence on multimember districts.

Changes in state chamber size affecting multimember district plans are interesting. One state, Illinois, reduced the size of its legislature by one-third and went from multimember to a single-district plan, factors that Wilma Rule assumed would undercut women's representation.[18] Niemi et al. would stipulate that such a plan should favor racial minorities, especially those in metropolitan areas. In a different example, Idaho's switch to multimember districts, and concomitant increase in chamber size, was deemed appropriate by the U.S. Supreme Court because it would increase Hispanic representation.[19] These factors tied to a reapportionment year during a major recession may blur out analysis, but I think that most multimember district plans will have a significant and positive effect on women's representation and perhaps on black representation.

Multimember districts seem to suggest that, at least for women, the competition for seats has an inverse relationship to representation. Multimember district plans seem to reduce competition for seats, although other factors associated with state environments might be at work. In large populous states with smaller chambers, women's representation might be hindered. Carol Nechemias notes, however, that women are successful in metropolitan areas.[20] The different findings, I think, have much to do with the different time frames each author is assessing. There is likely to be some ambiguity in these findings because some research indicates women are less competitive, an assumption I find difficult to accept. There may be some clear differences when one differentiates women as Democrats or Republicans because their constituencies are likely to be quite different.

Although minority representation and turnover are likely to vary from state to state, they may also vary over time. An election following reapportionment and during a deep recession may provide more opportunities for minority representation, especially Democratic representation. This election may reflect voter perceptions that Republicans are responsible for a downturn in the economy. But what effect will the 1984 presidential election have? Again, I think one can assume that Republicans might be able to do well riding the coattails of the very popular President Ronald Reagan. Although one can assume a swing in party fortunes affecting minorities, what impact will there be when more voters participate who may be less well educated and well-to-do? Will their participation slow the pace of women's increasing representation? And finally, in the 1986 off-year election where fewer voters participate, will women do better as a group? Will Hispanic and black representation possibly recede as fewer of their constituents vote? Again, the 1986 election, with the possible effect of the Iran-Contra scandal, may overshadow local issues and create opportunities favoring Democratic minorities. Nelson in a study of eight continental Hispanic states found that women's representation tended to slow and decline after the 1984 election. In these eight states, their representation never reached its 1983 high following the 1982 election.[21] For blacks, and to some extent Hispanics, their representation increased after the 1982 and 1984 elections. Perhaps one may posit that greater turnout will be a positive factor in their increased representation because far more blacks and Hispanics are likely to vote in a presidential election.

Finally, perhaps we can stipulate that there will be greater opportunities for these minorities if their states have institutionalized antidiscrimination legislation. Kwang Shik Shinn created an antidiscrimination index that rank ordered the states that had enacted legislation addressing a number of egalitarian issues. Among the important pieces of legislation he addressed were fair employment practices, equal pay, minimum wages, and racial, gender, and age discrimination in the public and private sectors.[22] I simply assume that states that first enacted statutes embodying values of antidiscrimination will represent more fertile ground for minority representation.

Party Factors

It has always been surprising that, more often than not, writers concerned about women's representation did not address the impact of political parties in a comparative perspective. If anything, party fortunes are likely to have an impact on minority representation. If legislatures change party control from Democratic to Republican, and vice versa, this should ideally have an important effect on their party members' political fortunes. During the 1980s, a number of states changed political hands. If women's representation as a whole does not change, there may be some trade-offs where Democratic women may win and Republican women may lose. Change in representation is "a wash," but change has occurred. Most studies that simply refer to women's representation neglect a simple fact that Republican and Democratic women and Hispanics are likely to be very different.[23]

The political fortunes of parties may provide an appealing incentive for their legislative members. Who controls a chamber and to what extent? A major reason for differentiating minorities by party membership is based on an assumption that a legislative seat is more appealing if one's party controls a legislative chamber. A legislator who wants to make a mark in life is likely to recognize that his or her potential influence in policy decisions is likely to be greater in the majority party. The majority has the most significant impact on the legislative agenda and on personnel decisions within party conferences and committee systems. Being a member of a majority party probably provides an additional incentive to remain in office and to seek office. Although an important political incentive, it may also be an impediment to new members. Incumbents in this favorable environment are unlikely to leave office and are not usually defeated. Wilma Rule has indicated that where the Democratic Party governs, women have less representation, and generally the Democrats have dominated most legislative chambers.[24] Incumbency due these conditions is one possible explanation for women's slow increase in legislative representation. Blacks and Hispanics seeking office for the first time could also face similar circumstances in their districts. But, if black and Hispanic voters have increased their numbers in a newly reapportioned district, then the incumbent who may not be black or Hispanic may be unseated. Voters tend to vote for legislators who mirror their racial, ethnic, and religious characteristics.[25]

Extreme party control (e.g., 75 percent or more of all seats controlled by the majority party) may have other consequences for the representation, turnover, and potential influence of minorities. In these circumstances, turnover among a bloated majority's side of the aisle may be quite large. It is feasible that a majority leadership may not need to address the interests of every majority party member in this situation. In a more competitive chamber, they may be more likely to respond to each member's interests in order to ensure the success of the majority party's bills. For the impotent minority party members, especially when there are so few of them, representation may remain low and turnover quite high. Summarizing, depending on the degree of party control, there may be more or less turnover among the majority party legislators. Minority party turnover is likely to be higher in any circumstance.

Local party effectiveness may also have an important effect on minorities. Although Darcy et al. indicate that local party organizations no longer appear to be important barriers to women, it would be interesting to ascertain what effect local parties do have on Democratic and Republican minority group success.[26] James L. Gibson et al. and David Mayhew have respectively identified effective local party organizations and traditional party organization states.[27] Do effective Democratic local party organizations have a significant effect on Republican minority representation? Similarly, what effect do local Republican party organizations have on Democratic minorities? Assuming that effective party organizations may be related to successful party representation, Gibson's rank order of both parties' local organizations may have a significant impact on minority representation and turnover. Again, one must differentiate minority party membership. The impact may be far more important for blacks and Hispanics depending on party control. If the majority party barely controls a chamber, it might be more willing to actively recruit blacks and Hispanics through local and perhaps state party organizations. Assessing the effects of traditional party organizations is difficult because they generally are metropolitan and have better legislative salaries.

Demographic Factors

A number of demographic factors may have an immense explanatory effect on minority representation. Because the electorate is likely to vote for politicians that reflect their ethnic, racial, and religious characteristics, the proportion of a state's population that is black or Hispanic is likely to predict the representation of each minority. If I had information on the proportion of Polish, Swedish, and other ethnic groups, ethnicity would probably predict women's representation as well. Unfortunately, these data do not exist in this analysis. (I would need the proportion of legislators, one group or another, as well as the proportion of a state's population in those ethnic groups.)

The metropolitan nature of a state is likely to have both negative and positive effects on our minority groups. For women as a group, metropolitan states have not been fruitful areas of their representation. This seems especially true of large Democratically controlled party organization states.[28] However, if I differentiate between Democratic and Republican women, will Democratic women, especially in the North, be represented in metropolitan states? What are the implications for Republican women? Blacks and Hispanics in the North are found in large metropolitan states. In the South, blacks live in both rural and metropolitan areas, and this could affect a southern regional analysis.

The differences between North and South go well beyond differences in black residential patterns. Although the South is changing, in the past women have found it a difficult region to obtain representation. In fact it is a unique cultural region. Past research by Nelson[29] and Diamond suggest that women's representation and potential influence is likely to be smaller in what Daniel J. Elazar would refer to as a traditionalistic subculture.[30] He indicated that political participation in the United States is shaped by three subcultures: moralistic, individualistic, and traditionalistic. The variation of women's representation is due in part to values governing "the kinds of people who become active in government and politics, as holders of elective offices, members of the bureaucracy, and active political workers."[31]

A moralistic subculture seems more open because citizens and leaders believe every citizen has the duty to participate in the healthy endeavor of politics. Members of states dominated by an individualistic subculture view politics as a dirty business, best left to professionals within a relatively strong party system (where women have not done well). The South's traditionalistic subculture emphasizes the maintenance of the existing order in which nonelites are not expected to be minimally involved in politics. Whereas Nelson found political culture to be significantly related to women's representation in the 1970s and 1980s,[32] new unpublished research found no significant relationship between Elazar's culture and women's representation following the 1986 election, although representation was much greater in the moralistic subculture.[33]

For this reason, one might reasonably assume that women's representation will be predicted by states with a dominant moralistic subculture. Black and Hispanic representation will probably be predicted by those states where their populations are relatively large: individualistic and traditionalistic states. The northern individualistic states are, after all, generally metropolitan. Women have not done well in these states, which are often traditional party organization states. These individualistic states are likely to predict the representation of blacks and Hispanics. And, traditionalistic states with their large black metropolitan and rural populations are also likely to predict black as well as Hispanic representation (especially in Florida, Texas, New Mexico, and Arizona).

Southern traditionalism also evokes images of white steepled churches of conservative Protestant sects. Religion is one aspect of politics that must be taken seriously when one assesses minority representation. A. Lewis Rhodes has reported that religion is a potent force affecting occupational choices. Such choices may be outside the eligibility pool of political recruitment affecting minority recruitment.[34] Kevin Phillips in his *Post-Conservative America* suggests that the United States may be going through a "fourth religious awakening." The conservative trends since the early 1970s and the realignment of the South toward the Republican Party in presidential elections is in part related to a "moral majority," conservative Protestant activism in U.S. politics.[35] Given the nature of social issues like abortion and school prayer, is it possible that the proportion of conservative Protestants and Roman Catholics might create a negative environment for minority representation in either party? I am assuming that the pervasive biblical bias against women may have important consequences for their representation.

There is evidence that the array of conservative Protestant sects included in this study, pentacostals, fundamentalists, and charismatics, dislike liberals, feminists and the perceived relationship to abortion, the women's liberation movement, and lesbian rights. Much of this opposition is due to religious beliefs but is likely to be translated into political preferences in the conservative 1980s. Charles Peek and Sharon Brown have found that political sex prejudice was high among white conservative Protestants, and there was a negative impact on black minorities. Using a different data set, Brian Powell and Lola Steelman found that fundamentalism did not predict a vote against women. Still, they found that female fundamentalism did predict sexism whereas male fundamentalism did not.[36] Although the evidence is mixed concerning the effect of conservative Protestants' votes against minorities, it would probably be wise to assume some effect. Cultural change is slow, and personal preferences conditioned over a lifetime do not dissipate entirely.

One could also add the proportion of Roman Catholics to this assessment as well. Do the strong biblical bias against women and a shared opposition to abortion and the Supreme Court's position on prayer in schools mean that the proportion of Roman Catholics and conservative fundamentalist Protestants will have negative consequences on female representation? Is it possible that Democratic female parity with their Republican peers was so long in coming given the opposition of conservative religious groups that have dominated the Democratic Party in the North and South? Does conservative fundamentalist Protestantism have a similar effect on black representation? I think one might be able to suggest that Roman Catholics as a proportion of a state might predict Hispanic representation, although it might have negative consequences for female Hispanics. Shortridge notes that one must differentiate between Roman Catholics of other ethnic backgrounds and super Roman Catholics associated with Hispanic and French populations.[37]

Of several demographic factors, a well-educated population and a large proportion of women employed in a state's economic work force should positively predict women's representation. Ideally, a highly educated population with 16 or more years of education should be more tolerant. In addition, a larger proportion of well-educated citizens vote. If they represent a larger proportion of the population, their impact is likely to be greater because voter participation has fallen to about 50 percent of the voting age population. A larger proportion of women employed should also predict greater acceptance of women's issues and be reflected in greater support for female candidates. Past research has indicated that if workers can enter the marketplace, two important things may occur. First, one might expect increased politicization, that is, greater political interest, issue awareness, political efficacy, and greater participation.

Second, group identification might be enhanced. One must be aware that different party attachments will preclude complete women's solidarity, but, at best, it should predict their political success. I am simply assuming that as more women are involved in the marketplace, they are likely to perceive women's issues and women candidates more favorably.[38] It may seem unlikely that these factors would predict black and Hispanic incorporation. However, if the marketplace has significantly created opportunities for women, there may be positive effects on minorities.

Finally, the nature of the educational systems in central cities or poor areas of the rural South and the low educational attainment in each might predict an inverse relationship with Hispanic and black minorities. An interesting problem is that metropolitan areas do predict female representation, and probably other minority success. If the proportion of well educated is lower in these areas, can we assume both positive and negative relationships between blacks and Hispanic genders and other women? In any case, it should be noted that the very few female black and Hispanic representatives make it difficult to differentiate the sexes as a proportion of chambers in this study. However, we may compare their representation with male representation within their respective political parties.

METHODOLOGY

The assessment of minority incorporation will focus on their representation, turnover, and potential influence within party leadership and as chairs of committees in 45 lower state legislative chambers. Nebraska is omitted because it has a unicameral legislature. Alabama, Louisiana, Maryland, and Mississippi are excluded because their lower chambers are elected to four-year terms, rather than two. Under these circumstances it becomes difficult to compare the implications of turnover to incorporation. Our dependent variables are the mean percent of Democratic and Republican females (other than Hispanic and black), blacks and Hispanics represented in chambers following three elections in 1982, 1984, and 1986. Further, I will assess the mean percent of turnover for each group in chambers, as well as indices of influence based on their party and committee chair positions.

Influence indices for each group will be based on party leadership positions and chairs held within the committee system. In 1987, Nelson created an index of women's potential influence easily applicable to any group in a state legislature.[39] The index was based on committee and leadership positions in 49 state legislative chambers following the 1984 election. A major criticism of this one-shot case study was the lack of longitudinal data that could determine whether women remained predictably "tracked" in human resource committees. Other peers suggested that the Nelson index had another shortcoming. It did not consider variations of political power based on partisan control of legislative chambers. The index used here includes partisan control but does not assess the effect of tenure, that is, does the minority member hold a committee position over time.[40] If one were to assess all members of the state legislative committee systems (outside the boundaries of this study), then the effect of tenure on minorities would be extremely valuable.

In the above discussion, my dependent variables are either the mean percent of minority legislators in chambers, the mean percent turnover within chambers, or indices of potential influence. There are also three policy variables: per capita expenditures for education, social and welfare services, and health and hospitals. In predicting these expenditures, my above dependent variables (measures of incorporation) also become independent variables. Twenty-four other independent variables represent my rather artificially created opportunity/incentive, party, and demographic factors. These independent variables represent either interval/ratio, ordinal, or dummy variables portraying an event or characteristic.

Among my opportunity/incentive independent variables, I have created several proportions that may reflect incentives or disincentives to minority legislators. In order to assess the effect of legislative salaries, I simply divided the per capita income of a state into the legislative salaries of each state. The salaries do not include additional living expenses or special pay for leaders. For states like Idaho, which pay $30 a day, this total was multiplied by the average session days during odd years. This is an effective statistic because one can compare ratios across states as different as Arkansas, Alaska, and California.[41] The effect of the number of legislative committee positions was determined in a similar manner. The number of standing legislative committee chairs was divided by the num-ber of legislators in each chamber. I assume the greater the proportion, the greater the incentive to remain in the legislature. Again, I assume that one remains in a legislative post in order to "make one's mark in life" and that this can be best done in a position of influence, for example, a committee chair.[42] I also tried to ascertain the effect of district size or competition for seats derived from a ratio of each state's voting age population divided by the number of seats in each chamber. The larger the ratio, the larger the constituency, and, if research is correct, fewer women might be represented in chambers with quite large constituencies.[43] It is more likely to reflect a positive relationship on black and Hispanic representation, certainly influence, in large metropolitan states. Of course, this blurs some differences in those states with a partial or total multimember district system.

Several other factors are constructed very differently. Kwang S. Shinn created a composite rank order index for states that had adopted antidiscriminatory policies over time. Those who passed these policies first were ranked first; those who adopted them much later were ranked last. I assume that states with early and strong institutional support for these policies will represent favorable environments for minority representation and influence. Finally, I have indicated that one reason for differentiating Republican and Democratic minority members was policy differences. Party fortunes could have a strong effect on incorporation. If a chamber's size is increased or reduced, it is coded as a dummy variable, and it could provide opportunities or disincentives to different minorities. Illinois is the only state during this period to reduce the size of its legislature and move from multimember districts to single-member district representation. Ideally, this should favorably affect black and Hispanic incorporation while possibly reducing female representation. Multimember district states are coded as dummy variables and should positively predict women's representation while possibly undercutting black and Hispanic representation in metropolitan areas.[44] Changes in party control coded as dummy variables will also affect minority influence depending on their party membership.

Finally, when assessing the effect of independent variables over the three election periods, there are dummy variables representing each election. I am assuming each election represents unique short-term events that may affect party fortunes. In 1982, a reapportionment and a recession affected party fortunes. If Lewis-Beck and Rice are correct, and the analysis can be extended to state legislative elections, the recession would be the most important factor and would harm Republican minorities.[45] The Republican presidential landslide in 1984 might have a salutary effect on Republican minorities whereas the off-year 1986 election, affected by the Iran-Contra affair and the Republican loss of the U.S. Senate, suggests a difficult year for state legislative Republicans. I think it important to note that the party-in-power in Washington, D.C., may at times represent a positive or negative voting cue for grassroots legislative voting and affect minority incorporation.

Among the party factors, James Gibson et al. created a rank order index assessing the organizational qualities of local Democratic and Republican parties from the best to the worst.[46] Uncertain about the impact of parties, I assumed local Democratic parties might have a negative effect on Democratic women given Rule's analysis.[47] I am very uncertain of local party organizations' effects on black and Hispanic representation. Do local party organizations have a positive or negative impact? In metropolitan areas are there significant black-white, Hispanic-white, or black-Hispanic conflicts that preclude any significant effect by local party organizations? And finally, what is the effect of an opposition party on incorporation? Does a strongly organized opposition party preclude challenges?

Other than local party organizations, the "traditional party organization" states represent a dummy variable in this analysis and may have an important negative impact on women's incorporation, especially Republican, and a positive environment (most traditional party organization states are metropolitan) for blacks and Hispanics.[48] Ideally, there should be less turnover in these states where politicians are "professional" and therefore have greater political influence.

Among the states where party control changed from Democrat or Republican (noted as dummy variables), partisan incorporation is likely to be affected. This may be less likely in black and Hispanic districts where voters probably elect representatives who share similar racial, ethnic, and religious characteristics. It would, however, affect their influence within the committee system. Finally, I have created an ordinal measure of party control from least Democratic to most Democratic. In many respects it is similar to Austin Ranney's index.[49] Ideally, party control should favor the minorities belonging to the majority.

The remaining eight demographic independent variables represent the proportion of the population living in metropolitan areas (central city and suburban), having 16 years of education or more, with employed females, and the proportions of the population that are black or Hispanic, and conservative Protestants or Roman Catholic. Only one of these, denoting states dominated by a moralistic subculture, is a dummy variable.

Metropolitan states with large black and Hispanic populations are likely to be the most important predictors of black and Hispanic incorporation. They are likely to be negatively related to women's representation, particularly Republican women. States whose populations are highly educated (and affluent by inference) with a large proportion of females formally employed in the economy are likely to be positively related to all women's representation, perhaps more so within Republican women who may represent a more affluent, better educated population. A moralistic political subculture is also likely to positively predict women's representation and influence. The impact of a moralistic subculture on other minority incorporation is likely to be negligible. Finally, the pervasive biblical bias against women among conservative Protestants is likely to have a negative relationship with all minorities.[50] Although Roman Catholicism is likely to be negatively related to women's incorporation, it is likely to be positively related to Hispanic incorporation. The possible impact of these variables on the problem of turnover is largely unknown.

I will use some rather simple descriptive statistics (mean percentages) to note changes in minority representation and turnover over time. This, however, is only a preliminary analysis. I want to use multiple regression analysis to isolate which independent variables best predict minority incorporation indices while controlling for all other independent variables. Specifically, I am interested in the R, the R square that represents the proportion of variance explained, and changes in the R square as new variables are added in each step. I will also report the *betas* because they indicate the relative strength each independent variable has in predicting the dependent variables.[51]

These statistics will be reported for the full period following the 1982, 1984, and 1986 elections. This strategy allows me to increase the number of cases from 45 to 135 and determine the effects of different elections on incorporation. In doing so, I will also be able to assess the cumulative impact of my independent variables nationally and, especially, regionally — North and South.

Finally, a note on the unique aspects of this research. I will be doing a longitudinal analysis that differentiates between Democratic and Republican minority members. There are three reasons for doing so. Differences between the majority and minority belie differences in terms of policy orientations, control of the legislature, and party fortunes. Democrats and Republicans may agree on broad, ambiguously stated goals, but the means to obtain these goals are often different. By a process of recruitment or self-selection, politicians are likely to be Democratic or Republican (obviously) and their constituencies different. Second, the emphasis on party success, especially as a majority party, has implica-tions for minority group influence. A majority party is likely to set a legislature's agenda, and, if a minority group belongs to the majority, they are likely to be more influential than those who do not. The minority party may play some role, to a greater or lesser degree, depending on the formal and normative rules that differ from state to state. Finally, party fortunes are tied to presidential party fortunes. As the Republican president's success surges and recedes in the public mind, so will the fortunes of his party in state legislative elections. These circumstances urge the differentiation between Democratic and Republican minority groups in addition to an assessment of each group without respect for party membership. Finally, the analysis of representation within parties is a different approach that should allow me to differentiate black and Hispanic males and female representation. These dependent variables represent the minorities representation as a proportion of their party's total membership. I think this analysis will reflect similar significant relationships found in analyses of minorities as a proportion of a chamber membership.

The remaining chapters address each of the three aspects of incorporation: representation, turnover, and personal influence. Chapter 2 concerns itself with representation within chambers; Chapter 3 focuses on representation within parties; Chapter 4 addresses turnover, and Chapter 5 addresses the real effects of representation on personal influence. Chapter 5 also assesses the effects of personal influence on policy outcomes, especially the per capita expenditures for education, welfare and social services, and health and hospitals. These are policy arenas where one may, given stereotypes and constituency needs, find minority influence to be dominant.

NOTES

1. Leonard A. Cole, *Blacks in Power: A Comparative Study of Black and White Elected Officials* (Princeton: Princeton University Press, 1976), pp. 37–55; R. Darcy, Susan Welch, and Janet Clark, *Women, Elections and Representation* (New York: Longman, 1967), Chapter 1; Susan Welch and John R. Hibbing, "Hispanic Representation in the U.S. Congress," in Rodolfo O. De la Garza et al., eds., *The Mexican-American Experience: An Interdisciplinary Anthology* (Austin: University of Texas Press, 1985), pp. 259–66; James Jennings and Monte Rivera, eds., *Puerto Rican Politics in Urban America* (Westport: Greenwood Press, 1984). In referring to representation, I am using Hanna Pitkin's *The Concept of Representation* (Berkeley: University of California Press, 1967), for the concept of "descriptive representation" rather than "substantive representation." In the former, one refers to legislators elected because they share the racial, ethnic, or religious attributes of constituents. Substantive representation, in part, suggests representation by one who may not share all these characteristics but does adequately represent constituent interests. The lists of females, blacks, and Hispanics represented in lower state legislative chambers were culled from a number of sources: Council of State Governments (CSG), *State Elective Officials and Legislatures*, 1983–1984; 1985–1986; and 1987–1988, *Supplement One, The Book of the States* (Lexington: CSG, 1983, 1985, 1987); Joint Center for Political Studies, *Directory of Black Leadership*, 1985 and 1987. (Washington, D.C.: Joint Center for Political Studies, 1985, 1987). Information concerning party leadership and committee chairs comes from CSG, *State Legislative Leadership, Committees and Staff* 1983–1984, 1985–1986, 1987–1988 (Lexington: CSG, 1983, 1985, 1987).

2. Rufus P. Browning, Dale Rogers Marshall, and David H. Tabb, *Protest Is Not Enough: The Struggle of Blacks and Hispanics for Equality in Urban Politics* (Berkeley: University of California Press, 1984), pp. 24–25, 240–41.

3. Joseph Schlesinger, *Ambition and Politics: Political Careers in the United States* (Chicago: Rand, McNally, 1966).

4. Elder Witt, "Are Our Governments Paying What It Takes to Keep the Best and Brightest?" *Governing* 2 (December 1988): 30–39; Peverill Squire, "Career Opportunities and Membership Stability in Legislatures," *Legislative Studies Quarterly* 13 (February 1988): 65–77.

5. Irene Diamond, *Sex Roles in the State House* (New Haven: Yale University Press, 1977); Wilma Rule, "Why Women Don't Run," *Western Political Quarterly* 34 (March 1984): 60–77.

6. Wayne L. Francis and James Riddlesperger, "U.S. State Legislative Committee Systems: Structure, Procedural Efficiency, and Party Control," *Legislative Studies Quarterly* 7 (November 1982): 453–71; Alan Rosenthal, *Legislative Life* (New York: Harper & Row, 1981), pp. 163–93 passim.

7. Rosenthal, ibid.; Keith E. Hamm and Ronald D. Hedlund, "Occupational Interests and State Legislative Committees," Paper delivered at the 1989 Annual Meeting of the Midwest Political Science Association, Chicago, Illinois.

8. Diamond, *Sex Roles*; Cole, *Blacks in Power*; Susan Gluck Mezey, "Does Sex Make a Difference?" *Western Political Quarterly* 31 (December 1978): 492–521; Ronnie More and Marvin Rich, "When Blacks Take Office," *Progressive* 36 (May 1972): 31.

9. Wayne L. Francis, "Agenda Setting and the Potential for Reciprocity in Legislatures," Paper presented at the 1986 Annual Meeting of the Midwest Political Science Association, Chicago, Illinois. Also see Kenneth A. Shepsle, *The Giant Jigsaw Puzzle: Democratic Committee Assignments in the Modern House* (Chicago: University of Chicago Press, 1978).

10. Richard Fenno, *Congressmen in Committees* (Boston: Little, Brown, 1973).

11. David R. Mayhew, *Congress: The Electoral Connection* (New Haven: Yale University Press, 1974), pp. 52–53.

12. Eric M. Uslaner and Ronald E. Weber, "U.S. State Legislators' Opinions of Constituency Attitudes," *Legislative Studies Quarterly* 4 (November 1979): 536–86; Robert Weisberg, "Assessing Legislator-Constituency Policy Agreement," *Legislative Studies Quarterly* 4 (November 1979): 605–22; John Kingdon, *Congressmen's Voting Decisions* (New York: Harper & Row, 1982); David Ray, "The Sources of Voting Cues in Three State Legislatures," *Journal of Politics* 44 (1982): 1074–87; Warren E. Miller and Donald E. Stokes, "Constituency Influence in Congress," *American Political Science Review* 57 (March 1973): 45–56; Robert S. Erickson, Norman Luttbeg, and William V. Holloway, "Knowing One's District: How Legislators Predict Referendum Voting," *American Journal of Political Science* 19 (1975): 231–46.

13. Diamond, *Sex Roles*; Marjorie R. Hershey, "The Politics of Androgyny: Sex Roles and Attitudes toward Women in Politics," *American Politics Quarterly* 5 (July 1977): 216–87; Nicholas Lehmann, "The Origins of the Underclass," *The Atlantic Monthly*, June 1986, pp. 31–55; James Fallows, "Immigration: How It's Affecting Us," *The Atlantic Monthly*, November 1983, pp. 45–106.

14. James Heilbrun, *Urban Economics and Public Policy* (New York: St. Martin's Press, 1982); Dennis R. Judd, *The Politics of American Cities* (Boston: Little, Brown, 1988), see especially pp. 229–53; see Susan J. Carroll, *Women as Candidates in American Politics* (Bloomington: Indiana University Press, 1985), for a partial list of feminist issues, pp. 148–49; see James Tobin, "Reaganomics in

Retrospect," in B. B. Kymlicka and Jean V. Matthews, eds., *The Reagan Revolution?* (Chicago: Dorsey Press, 1988), pp. 85–103, for the Reagan administration's blind spots concerning the nation's social urban crisis.

15. Charles S. Bullock III, "Congressional Voting and Mobilization of a Black Electorate in the South," *Journal of Politics* 43 (1981): 662–82; I. A. Lewis and William Schneider, "Black Voting, Bloc Voting, and the Democrats," *Public Opinion* 6 (1983): 12–15; Frederick Harris and Linda Williams, "JCPS/Gallup Poll Reflects Changing Views on Political Issues," *Focus* 14 (1986): 3–6; Ford Foundation, *Hispanics: Challenges and Opportunities* (New York: Ford Foundation, 1984); Fred R. Harris, *American Democracy* (Glenview: Scott-Foresman, 1986), pp. 161–64; Guadalupe San Miguel, "Conflict and Controversy in the Evolution of Bilingual Education in the United States — An Interpretation," in De la Garza et al., eds., *Mexican-American Experience*; Jennings and Rivera, eds., *Puerto Rican Politics*.

16. Shayne Merritt, "Sex Roles and Political Ambition," *Sex Roles* 8 (September 1982): 1035; also see Christine De Stefano, "Postmodernism/ Postfeminism," Paper presented at the 1987 Annual Meeting of the American Political Science Association, Chicago, Illinois; see a fine bibliographic essay by Wilma Rule Kraus, "Political Implications of Gender Roles: A Review of the Literature," *American Political Science Review* 68 (December 1974): 1706–23; Virginia Sapiro, *The Political Integration of Women* (Urbana: University of Illinois Press, 1983); Diamond, *Sex Roles*; Hershey, "Politics of Androgyny"; Jeanne Kirkpatrick, *Political Woman* (New York: Basic Books, 1977); Kim Frederick Kahn and Edie N. Goldenberg, "Evaluations of Male and Female U.S. Senate Candidates," Paper presented at the 1988 Annual Meeting of the Midwest Political Science Association, Chicago, Illinois; Jack R. Van der Slik neatly addresses differences in his "Legislative Performance: Comparing Aspirations, Styles and Achievements of Women and Men Members of the Illinois General Assembly," Paper presented at the 1988 Annual Meeting of the Midwest Political Science Association, Chicago, Illinois. For women's past involvement in social welfare policy, I must refer to the fine presentation of Dr. Brad Yoder, "Social Welfare in the United States before 1914," Presentation at the National Endowment for the Humanities Summer Seminar on the American Regulatory and Social Welfare State, Vanderbilt University, July 1, 1988. See Jane Addams, *Twenty Years at Hull House* (New York: New American Library, 1961 [1910]); June Axinn and Hermann Levin, *Social Welfare: A History of the American Response to Need* (New York: Harper & Row, 1982); Roy Lubove, *The Professional Altruist: The Emergence of Social Work as a Career 1880–1930* (Cambridge: Harvard University Press, 1965); see some chapters in Herbert Stroup, *Social Welfare Pioneers* (Chicago: Nelson-Hall, 1986); Walter I Trattner, *From Poor Law to Welfare State* (New York: Free Press, 1979).

17. R. Darcy, Susan Welch, and Janet Clark, *Women, Elections, and Representation* (New York: Longman, 1987), p. 38; Richard G. Niemi and Laura Winsky, "Membership Turnover in the U.S. State Legislatures," *Legislative Studies Quarterly* 12 (February 1987): 115–24.

18. Rule, "Why Women Don't Run"; Niemi, et al., "Membership Turnover."

19. *Hellar v. Cenarusa,* 682p.2d524; 1984.

20. See Darcy et al., *Women, Elections, and Representation*; Rule, "Why Women Don't Run"; Carol Nechemias, "Geographic Mobility and Women's Access to State Legislatures," *Western Political Quarterly* 38 (March 1985): 119–31, reported by

Darcy et al., disagrees with Rule about the barriers provided by metropolitan attributes. Her study indicates that women do well in metropolitan areas.

21. Albert J. Nelson, "Representation and Turnover of Women, Blacks, and Hispanics in Eight States," Paper presented at the 1989 Annual Meeting of the Midwest Political Science Association, Chicago, Illinois. Of course, I was aware that unique local issues and changes especially in Illinois might have some very real impact on these states. Although a heuristic study, this analysis should give a far better idea of how well minorities are doing in the three election years. In using this approach, my analysis reflects the work of John F. Bibby, "Pattern of Midterm Gubernatorial and State Legislative Elections," *Public Opinion Quarterly* 6 (1983): 41–46; and James E. Campbell, "Presidential Coattails and Midterm Losses in State Legislative Elections," *American Political Science Review* 80 (March 1986): 45–64.

22. Kwang Shik Shinn, *Innovation Adoption and Diffusion in the Political System of States: A Focus on Taxation and Antidiscrimination* (Carbondale: Ph.D. dissertation written at Southern Illinois University, 1979).

23. See Carroll, *Women as Candidates,* who assesses significant differences between Democratic and Republican women on feminist issues. They may share similar goals (equality, for example), but the means to obtain them may be quite different.

24. Rule, "Why Women Don't Run."

25. Thomas R. Dye, "State Legislative Politics," in Herbert Jacob and Kenneth N. Vines, eds., *Politics in the American States* (Boston: Little, Brown, 1965), p. 106.

26. Darcy et al., *Women, Elections, and Representation,* p. 38.

27. James L. Gibson et al., "Whither the Local Parties?" *American Journal of Political Science* 29 (February 1985): 139–60; David R. Mayhew, *Placing Parties in American Politics* (Princeton: Princeton University Press, 1986). In my analysis of traditional party organization states, those specified *four* and *five* (strong traditional party organization states) by Mayhew are given a value of "1" in my data analysis. All other states are given the value of zero.

28. Rule, "Why Women Don't Run."

29. Albert J. Nelson, "Women's Advancement as Chairpersons: 1979 and 1983," *International Journal of Intercultural Relations* 4 (1987): 401–10; and his "Political Culture and Women's Representation in Lower State Legislatures," *International Journal of Intercultural Relations* 4 (1980): 367–77; "Women's Potential Influence in Lower State Legislative Chambers, 1985 to 1986," *Wisconsin Political Scientist* 2 (Fall 1987); Diamond, *Sex Roles.*

30. See Daniel J. Elazar, *American Federalism: A View from the States* (New York: Thomas Y. Crowell, 1972); and see the interesting assessment of cultural regions by Raymond D. Gastil, *Cultural Regions of the United States* (Seattle: University of Washington Press, 1975).

31. Elazar, *American Federalism,* p. 112.

32. See Nelson, 1980, "Political Culture"; 1987, "Women's Advancement," in *International Journal of Intercultural Relations.*

33. Albert J. Nelson, "Decline of Elazar's Cultural Concept in Explaining Women's Representation," Unpublished paper at the University of Wisconsin — LaCrosse, 1988. The findings of the one-way analysis of variance measuring the effects of the 1986 election is as follows:

Source of Variation	df	SS	MS	F/ratio	p
Between Groups	2	275.4	137.7	1.903	< .16
Within Groups	46	3328.1	72.4		
Total	48	3603.5			

Culture	n	means	SD
Moralistic	17	13.75%	11.2
Individualistic	15	8.67	7.0
Traditionalistic	17	8.86	6.3

The findings indicate that women's representation in the South has slightly surpassed their representation in northern individualistic dominated states. However, their representation is greater in moralistic states as Diamond, *Sex Roles*, indicated it should be. For this reason, moralistic subculture will represent the single dummy cultural variable that should ideally predict women's representation. Black and Hispanic representation is likely to fall in the individualistic and traditionalistic states where their populations are quite large.

34. A. Lewis Rhodes, "Effects of Religious Denominations in Occupational Choices," *Sex Roles* 9 (January 1983): 93–108. This dovetails with Susan Welch's analysis of eligibility pools, "Recruitment of Women to Public Office: A Discriminant Analysis," *Western Political Quarterly* 31 (September 1978): 372–80.

35. Kevin Phillips, *Post-Conservative America* (New York: Random House, 1982).

36. Charles W. Peek and Sharon Brown, "Sex Prejudice among White Protestants: Like or Unlike Ethnic Prejudice," *Social Forces* 59 (September 1980): 169–85; Brian Powell and Lola Carr Steelman, "Fundamentalism and Sexism: A Reanalysis of Peek and Brown," *Social Forces* 60 (June 1982): 1154–67; Ernest Wollenberg, "Correlates of the Equal Rights Amendment," *Social Science Quarterly* 60 (March 1980): 676–84. Peek and Brown used data on fundamentalists found in Rodney Stark and Charles Y. Glock, *American Piety: The Nature of Religious Commitment* (Berkeley: University of California Press, 1968). Clyde Wilcox and Elizabeth Adell Cook, "Evangelical Women and Feminism," *Women and Politics* 9 (1989): 27–49; Clyde Wilcox, "Lingering Support for the Christian Right: Robertson and Christian Right Groups in 1988," Paper delivered at the 1990 Annual Meeting of the Midwest Political Science Association, Chicago, Illinois. A number of authors have reported that existing "regional religious peculiarities and differences remain important in spite of the homogenization of America." See Samuel S. Hill, "Religion and Region in America," *The Annals* 480 (July 1985): 132–41; Wilbur Zelinsky, "An Approach to Religious Geography in the United States: Patterns of Church Membership in 1952," *Annals of the Association of American Geographers* 51 (June 1981): 133–93; James R. Shortridge, "A New Regionalization of American Religion," *Journal for the Scientific Study of Religion* 16 (June 1977): 143–54. In my study, the conservative Protestant groups as a proportion of state populations are Baptists, Assembly of God, all Brethren's, Church of Christ except the United Church of Christ, all Evangelicals, all Holiness Groups, Jehovah's Witnesses, Nazarene, all Pentecostals, Seventh Day Adventists, and Missionary Baptists found in Bernard Quinn et al., *Churches and Church Membership in the U.S., 1980* (Atlanta: Glenmary Research Center, 1982). It should be noted that the black churches are not reported in

this publication and that the numbers of Roman Catholic communicant members is usually overstated by the Roman Catholic Church.

37. Shortridge, "New Regionalization."

38. Kristi Anderson, "Working Women and Political Participation, 1952–1972," *American Journal of Political Science* 19 (August 1975): 439–53. Anderson's research indicates that employed females were more likely to identify themselves as liberals than were housewives. Although this might suggest the possibility of a woman's political party, Anderson indicates that "women are probably too crosspressured ever to constitute a lasting political movement," p. 452. For increased politicization, see Robert A. Dahl, *After the Revolution?* (New Haven: Yale University Press, 1970); William H. Flanigan and Nancy H. Zingale, *Political Behavior and the American Electorate* (Boston: Allyn and Bacon, 1970; 1987); Carole Pateman, *Participation and Democratic Theory* (Cambridge: Cambridge University Press, 1970).

39. Albert J. Nelson, "Women's Political Influence within Lower State Legislative Chambers," Paper presented at the 1987 Annual Meeting of the Midwest Political Science Association, Chicago, Illinois; and "Women's Potential Influence in Lower State Legislative Chambers," *Wisconsin Political Scientist* 2 (Fall 1987): 5–13.

40. This idea is much like the concept of "constancy" found in Ronald D. Hedlund and Dianne Powers, "Constancy of Committee Membership in 16 States: 1971 to 1986," Paper presented at the 1987 Annual Meeting of the Midwest Political Science Association, Chicago, Illinois. It should be noted that this constancy is crucial to the professional institutionalization of state legislatures. See Nelson W. Polsby, "The Institutionalization of the U.S. House of Representatives," *American Political Science Review* 63 (March 1968): 787–807.

41. This will certainly take care of differences in cost of living in states as different as Alaska, Arkansas, and New York, and it allows comparisons. See Witt, "Are Our Governments Paying?" for data on salaries; and the U.S. Bureau of Census, *County and City Data Book* (Washington, D.C.: U.S. Government Printing Office, 1983), for per capita income and a number of other demographic variables.

42. See Squire, "Career Opportunities," for this idea. The data on committees is found in Council of State Governments, *State Legislative Leadership, Committees and Staff, 1983, 1985, 1987* (Lexington: CSG, 1983, 1985, 1987).

43. Rule, "Why Women Don't Run."

44. Niemi et al., "Membership Turnover."

45. Michael S. Lewis-Beck and Tom W. Rice, "Forecasting U.S. House Elections," *Legislative Studies Quarterly* 9 (November 1984): 475–86; and Michael S. Lewis-Beck, "Election Forecasts in 1984: How Accurate Were They?" *PS* 18 (Winter 1985): 53–62. See Campbell, "Presidential Coattails," and Bibby, "Pattern of Midterm Gubernatorial."

46. Gibson et al., "Whither the Local Parties?"

47. Rule, "Why Women Don't Run."

48. Mayhew, *Placing Parties in American Politics.*

49. Austin Ranney, "Parties in State Politics," in Herbert Jacob and Kenneth N. Vines, eds., *Politics in the American States,* pp. 51–92. The ranges are (1) 0 to 24% Democrat; (2) 25 to 40% Democrat; (3) 41 to 49.9% Democrat; (4) 50.1 to 60% Democrat; (5) 61 to 75% Democrat; (6) 76% plus Democrat; (7) 50% Democrat and Republican (Montana one election's effect).

50. Peek and Brown, "Sex Prejudice."

51. Michael S. Lewis-Beck, *Applied Regression: An Introduction* (Beverly Hills: Sage, 1980); Norman H. Nie et al., *SPSSx* (New York: McGraw-Hill, 1986); Edward R. Tufte, *The Quantitative Analysis of Social Problems* (Reading, Mass.: Addison-Wesley, 1970.

2

MINORITY REPRESENTATION IN CHAMBERS

Membership — getting into the legislature and remaining there — is an important first step of incorporation. Necessarily, a legislator has to remain for some time to obtain the necessary policy expertise and understand the complex rules and procedures that enhance legislative success. I assume that the success of a minority group is linked in part to what percentage it represents in a chamber, and I believe it is important that representation be in the majority party.

Minority incorporation varies over time nationally and in different regions. This is portrayed in Tables 2.1 and 2.2. One should be cognizant that changes in representation, whether ebbing or increasing, represent very minute percentages. Therefore, caution is advisable because assessing trends under these conditions is difficult.

DESCRIBING MINORITY REPRESENTATION

Women's Representation

Women's representation (excluding blacks and Hispanics) seems relatively stable, but when one differentiates Democratic and Republican women, there have been relatively important shifts in representation. Nationally, their representation as a single group rises from 14.4 percent in 1983, expands to 15.1 percent after the presidential election in 1984, and sags to 15.0 percent in 1987. These shifts mask the effect of changing party fortunes, I think, tied to the pulse of presidential success.[1] Nationally, Democratic women's representation continues to creep upward from 7.4 percent to 7.8 percent regardless of presidential

TABLE 2.1
Women's Mean Percent Representation in Lower State Legislative Chambers, by Region

		Region	
Year	National	North	South
1983			
All Women*	14.4	15.9	9.1
Democrats	7.4	7.5	6.8
Republicans	7.0	8.4	2.3
1985			
All Women*	15.1	16.8	9.5
Democrats	7.5	7.8	6.6
Republicans	7.6	9.0	2.9
1987			
All Women*	15.0	16.5	10.1
Democrats	7.8	8.3	6.2
Republicans	7.2	8.2	3.9

*All women except blacks and Hispanics.

success. Republican female representation expands from 7.0 in 1983 and surpasses Democratic female representation at 7.6 percent in 1985. However, it falls with party fortunes to 7.2 percent after the 1986 election when Republicans lost control of the United States Senate.

Regionally, all women's representation rises, then falls in the North, but it continues to rise in the South where women's representation has always lagged. Although some academicians believe that incumbency is one factor affecting women's political stagnation in state legislatures, they neglect the effects of presidential success on legislative elections. Republican representation in the North follows the pulse of presidential success. Their representation increases from 8.4 percent in 1983 to 9.0 percent in 1987; then it falls with Republican fortunes to 8.2 percent in 1987.[2] However, southern Republican women's representation seems unaffected by presidential fluctuations. Their representation increased every election from 2.3 percent in 1983 to 3.9 percent in 1987. Democratic representation in the South slowly ebbs from 6.8 percent to 6.2 percent while it rises sluggishly from 7.4 to 7.8 percent without regard to presidential success in either region. One must question whether better educated (and affluent?) areas in the South are slowly realigning in legislative elections and cutting into former Democratic districts represented by women. In any case, the sluggish national representation of women belies changes affected by party success in different regions.

Black and Hispanic Representation

Black and Hispanic representation is relatively stable, although one can see some movement in Table 2.2. Nationally, black representation rises from 4.1 percent in 1983 to 4.4 percent in 1985 and ever so slightly declines to 4.3 percent in 1987. Table 2.2 indicates that most black representation lies in the South, and it continues to advance with each election. It remains highly stable in the North at 3.5 percent, although it imperceptibly fell in 1987 (the percentages are rounded off to the nearest tenth). Hispanic representation is quite small, but this is to be expected because very few Hispanics are registered to vote. For this reason,

TABLE 2.2

Mean Percent Representation of Blacks and Hispanics in Lower State Legislative Chambers, by Region

	Region		
Year	National	North	South
1983			
Black Democrats	4.1	3.5	6.7
All Hispanics	1.8	1.9	1.5
Democrats	1.6	1.7	1.2
Republicans	.2	.2	.3
1985			
Black Democrats	4.4	3.5	7.4
All Hispanics	2.0	2.2	1.6
Democrats	1.6	1.8	1.0
Republicans	.4	.4	.6
1987			
Black Democrats	4.3	3.5	7.5
All Hispanics	2.0	1.9	2.3
Democrats	1.7	1.7	1.7
Republicans	.3	.2	.6

Hispanic representation has hardly increased nationally, whether one assesses Democratic or Republican members. Regionally, there are some differences. Initially, Hispanic representation is greater in the North where it slowly increases from 1.9 percent in 1983 to 2.2 percent in 1985. It then slumps to 1.9 percent in 1987. Much of this variation is due to Republican Hispanics whose success is tied to the Republican administration. In the South, Hispanic representation continues to move upward from 1.5 percent in 1983 to 2.3 percent in 1987. It appears that both Democratic and Republican success is directly related to party fortunes, quite unlike the trends found among Democratic and Republican women in the South. Again, one must be quite cautious because the percentages are so small that it is difficult to specify significant shifts in Hispanic representation. I believe one can presume that their representation is likely to increase in the twenty-first century when a larger proportion will be registered to vote.

EXPLAINING MINORITY REPRESENTATION

National Variations — All Women

The explanation of women's representation focuses on multiple regression analysis. In the below analyses, we focus on three statistical measures: the R square, *beta* weights, and the T-test. An R square represents the proportion of variance in minority representation explained by all our independent variables. The higher the R square, the more complete our explanation of representation, turnover, or potential influence (i.e., incorporation). The relative importance of each independent variable is found in *beta* weights, that is, "the average standard deviation change in [minority representation] is associated with a standardized change in [each independent variable], when other independent variables are held constant."[3] The greater the *beta* weight, the greater the impact of the independent variable in minority indices of incorporation. Finally, the choice of which *beta* weights to emphasize is related to a T-test significance of each independent variable. The focus is on the most significant (sig. < .001) to marginally significant (sig. < .10). This latter level of significance is reported for one reason: as in most correlational analyses, there is a good deal of interpretive ambiguity. A different research strategy focusing on another level of analysis might find these marginal independent variables important enough to utilize. It is assumed that not all independent variables will significantly predict minority representation.

Initially, I will focus on women as a group (excluding Hispanics and blacks) for one specific purpose — the symbolic importance of representing an important, although often overlooked, segment of the population. Women in state legislatures have symbolic importance, but with specific political party identification, they have varying degrees of power. But first, let me assess those state attributes that seem to predict their representation in the 1980s.

Twenty-two independent variables predict 41, 41, and 40 percent of the variance for all women, Democratic women, and Republican women's representation (Table 2.3). Six variables consistently and significantly predict women's representation: percent females employed in the work force, percent of the population with 16 years or more education, percent population in metropolitan areas, percent Roman Catholic, percent conservative Protestants, and historical support for antidiscrimination statutes. Two other variables (legislative salary ratio and the efficacy of local Democratic party organizations) have an effect on one or two of these independent variables.

As expected, although not in terms of its primacy, the proportion of women employed is a major predictor of all women's representation (*beta* .52). Academics have speculated that as more women enter the labor force, they are likely to become more interested in political issues and

TABLE 2.3

Multiple Regression Analyses' *Betas* **of Women's National Representation in Three Elections**

Independent Variables	All Women*	Democrats	Republicans
Females Employed	.52 a	.41 a	.60 a
Educ. 16 Years +	−.45 a	−.44 a	−.44 a
Metropolitan Pop.	.41 a	.40 b	.40 b
Roman Catholic	−.39 a	−.37 b	−.39 b
Cons. Protestants	−.36 b	−.42 a	−.29 c
Antidiscrimination	−.29 c	−.31 c	−.26 c
Local Democratic Orgns.	.27 c	.33 b	.20 NS
Legislative Salary	−.18 NS	−.24 c	−.13 NS
R square	.41	.41	.40

Notes:

Reports only those *betas* that are significant for one or all groups of women.

a = T-test sig. < .001; b = T-test sig. < .01; c = T-test sig. < .05; d = T-test sig. < .10; NS = not significant.

*All women except blacks and Hispanics.

participate. In addition, I think that their marketplace responsibilities will engender a climate that may also accept women as political candidates. As the life experiences of women increase, not only do men change their assessment of women, perhaps of more importance, women may change their personal appraisals. It would seem likely that their behavior should positively affect other women's expectations of their roles in society. Kristi Anderson has pointed out attitudinal differences between working women and housewives.[4] Working women's attitudes toward politics and participation seemed more liberal, probably because of their experiences in the workplace. The changes wrought by work experiences enhance different expectations in what environments women can be fully productive. In fact, one must stipulate that employed females obtain political interest and efficacy and that these attitudes lead to participation in politics.

However, if more women working is an expected predictor of women's representation, the inverse relationship between the proportion of the population with 16 or more years of education (*beta* −.45) and women's representation is unexpected. I would assume that states with a greater percentage of skilled, professionally educated citizens would be fertile environments for women's political success. Darcy et al. note that as women enter professional occupations, especially law, their representation has increased accordingly.[5] Although this independent variable is not a similar measure, I had assumed a well-educated populace would have a positive impact on women's representation. I implicitly assumed that there would be a positive relationship between education and increased tolerance. Perhaps this relationship is in part due to the attributes of low educational attainment within larger metropolitan states.

In earlier analyses of women's representation, research indicated that metropolitan states and their large legislative districts were hostile environments for women's political success.[6] However, this analysis agrees with Carol Nechemias that metropolitan characteristics do indeed predict women's representation (*beta* .41).[7] What makes this even more important is that Hispanic and black females are not counted in this dependent variable. Both groups' representatives are likely to be found in large northern, metropolitan states; hence, they are not skewing the findings. I believe that findings that found metropolitan areas a barrier to women's success were historically correct. There is really no serious conflict between Nechemias, the findings of this study, and the writers whose data were based on the 1960 and 1970 decades. The glacial advance of women during the 1980s may have much to do with a shift to a larger electoral base whose heterogeneity makes rapid advances far more difficult than they might be in homogeneous, sparsely populated states. Women's early success in these states also meant that a moralistic subculture was likely to predict women's success.[8] This is not true in the 1980s. If this trend of representation continues and voters further adjust to female candidates, it is likely that women's representation will continue to grow, perhaps at a more rapid rate in the 1990s. Part of this growth will be due to what I perceive to be the somewhat greater moderation of President George Bush's administration compared to President Ronald Reagan's. As the administration's more moderate course develops, greater encouragement for women's political role is also likely to develop. My reasoning is quite simple. I think that participation is more likely if positive responses to women's issues exist, that is, the administration's more moderate course may lead to the development of policies associated with some, although not all, women's policy preferences.

Two barriers that affect women's representation belong to cultural biases found in U.S. culture: conservative Protestantism and Roman Catholicism. The pervasive biblical bias against women has been found to affect their occupational choices, and as a result, certainly political representation.[9] This study verifies that conservative Protestantism has a significant inverse relationship (*beta* $-.36$) with women's representation. The dislike for feminists and their probable relationship to abortion issues is in part responsible for this relationship. To this I must add that the proportion of the population that is Roman Catholic also inversely predicts (*beta* $-.39$) their representation. Conservative Protestantism and Roman Catholicism's political effect is in part due to the conservative Reagan era, which has espoused a number of conservative social issues, for example, pro-life position on abortion, and realistically provided negative reinforcement for women's political involvement. The repercussions of this conservative era reveal a coalition of Roman Catholicism and conservative Protestantism, at least on some conservative social issues. The upshot of this relationship may be to identify female candidates that support social issues like abortion and oppose them. Although not all female politicians reflect support for feminist issues, religious groups such as these are critical "gate keepers" in the political system.[10] Strong adherents of these religious sects may not be majorities within districts, but they can represent an important bloc of voters opposed to candidates with more liberal leanings, or perhaps they will oppose female candidates who do not perform stereotypical roles such as wives, mothers, and homemakers.[11] I think it is important to remember cultural values that stereotype women in nurturing roles remain in place today. A CBS/*New York Times* poll of attitudes in 1984 found "general agreement among all groups that on compassion, protecting the needy, women are better [than men] by margins of four and five to one."[12]

Although these biases exist, one major facilitator of women's representation is an early history of strong antidiscrimination legislation. States with a longer record of social and economic antidiscrimination statutes on the books are far more likely to predict (*beta* −.29) women's representation.[13] Perhaps the importance of the variable is reflected in the percent of women in the work force. It is obvious that some states earlier responded to women's movement into the work force, or perhaps the legislation is due to sensitivity to minority efforts to enter the work force. I think in large part the rights revolution has had an immense spillover impact on women's employment opportunities. What was intended to positively affect black opportunity has also had significant impact on women's representation.

Darcy et al. indicate that party organizations no longer prove to be barriers to women's representation, but it is interesting to note that weak, local Democratic party organizations are more likely to predict (*beta* .27) women's success.[14] Wilma Rule's study in 1984 indicated that the Democratic Party's impact was to undermine women's political ambition.[15] This relationship indicates that women are likely to do better if local Democratic organizations are not particularly efficacious.

National Variations — Partisan Differences

The ideological differences between Democratic and Republican women reported by Carroll represent one reason why one should differentiate women's representation by party.[16] In addition, one may assume some basic constituent differences that would predict their representation. This methodological approach is likely to provide alternative explanations of women's representation that might be obscured by simply grouping all women together.

There are some subtle differences between Democrats and Republicans, although the similarities in the findings here are quite remarkable. Generally, both multiple regression analyses explain nearly the same proportion of variance: 41 percent for Democrats and 40 percent for Republicans. Among Democratic women, four independent variables are closely clustered in predicting their representation. In roughly the order of the strength of the predictors (*beta* weights), the proportion of the population with 16 years or more education is inversely related (*beta* −.44). This might be expected because the traditional elements of the Democratic Party have not been the better educated or affluent. However, the impact of metropolitan state attributes (*beta* .40) emphasizes a degree of interpretive ambiguity. One is likely to find large groups of poorly educated in large metropolitan states. Nevertheless, these same states with their advanced economies should also be an environment where a large percentage of well-educated professionals are likely to be found, especially in the important growing service industries in finance, government, and law. Conditionally, some elements of lower-class status should not be overlooked because the proportion of women in the marketplace (*beta* .41) does not predict female Democratic representation as strongly as it does for all women or Republicans.

The barriers provided by religious groups, conservative Protestantism (*beta* −.42) and Roman Catholicism (*beta* −.37), are quite significant for a party traditionally tied to the South (not in presidential elections, but still crucial in state and local elections) and metropolitan states with large Roman Catholic, ethnic populations. First, Wilma Rule found that where Democrats are represented in strength, women's political success in state legislatures is likely to be lower.[17] The reason, during this conservative era, is that Democratic women face difficult barriers within their traditional constituencies: Roman Catholic ethnics and white, conservative Protestants. Perhaps this is due in part to the pervasive biblical bias against women, and opposition to liberal Democratic women exists over issues like abortion. And, I believe, this is reflected in the impact of local Democratic party organizations on their representation. If local Democratic organizations are weak (*beta* .33), there will likely be more women in state legislatures. In addition, the antidiscrimination index (*beta* −.31) is important. The early enactment of social-economic-political antidiscrimination statutes is an environmental facilitator of Democratic women's representation.

Although no association has been found between the incentive of a good legislative salary and women's national representation, it does play a significant role (*beta* −.24) for Democratic women, but not for other women. These variables do raise some questions of interpretive ambiguity often found in correlational analyses. If women are politically successful in large metropolitan states, does a central city or suburban population predict their representation? What kind of suburb — blue collar or white collar? The indications are that Democratic females' representation sharply increases in large metropolitan states; Republican representation is great in nonmetropolitan and large metropolitan states with moderate representation in those states between.

Republican women's representation is predicted by fewer factors, and there is some difference between them. Still, the predominant variables in the earlier analyses remain significant. First, like the analysis of all women, the proportion of women employed in the economy is the major predictor (*beta* .60) of Republican female political success. In those states where women are more likely to be working, Republican success is greater, suggesting at least more tolerant attitudes toward women's participation outside the home.[17] The greater employment opportunities for more affluent Republican women has had a greater effect on their participation. This does not mean that Republican women are likely to be more liberal on women's issues. One might infer this by the smaller effect (with respect to Democratic females) of conservative Protestants as a barrier to female Republican representation (*beta* −.29). I think one may assume that the conservative movement associated with the Republican Party means a less negative impact, albeit still a significant barrier, to female Republicans. Surprisingly, the proportion of the population with 16 years or more of education remains a significant predictor of Republican representation (*beta* −.44). This is probably due in part to the metropolitan attributes of states that also predict (*beta* .40) their representation. Again, there is ambiguity here. Generally, Democrats do well in large, metropolitan areas, and Republicans do not. Perhaps we are really dealing with different populations in metropolitan areas, the suburbs, but this well-educated, affluent outer ring of the central cities is lost in the analysis. To support this thesis, the inverse relationship with Roman Catholicism (*beta* −.39) is politically appropriate. Generally, when one refers to Republican opposition, one refers to Roman Catholic ethnics, especially in the North. Republican support is likely among Protestants, although, as my findings indicate, not among conservative fundamentalists.

Much like the analysis of all women and Democrats, the antidiscrimination index significantly predicts (*beta* −.26) Republican representation. Again, the historical development of antidiscrimination laws affecting private sector employment and citizenship rights is important to Republican women's success. I would reiterate that the passage of legislation to protect black minorities has also had a significant effect on all women who are not black. The states that lagged in passing a wide range of statutes associated with the rights revolution are those that are less likely to elect women candidates.

Northern Variations — All Women

Differences between North and South must always be considered in any analysis of political representation.[19] At first glance, the analysis of women's representation in the North mirrors in some ways the findings above (Table 2.4). This is true whether the dependent variables include all women (except blacks and Hispanics) or are differentiated by their partisan attachments.

The multiple regression analysis of all women's representation in the North explains 47 percent of the variance. Of the 22 independent variables in this study, the most important predictor is the proportion of females employed (*beta* .57). Like the assessment of national variations, this remains an important predictor of women's representation. The similarity of this analysis is enhanced by the importance of four other variables: percent of the population that has 16 or more years of education (*beta* −.41), metropolitan state attributes (*beta* .36), the effect of antidiscrimination statutes (*beta* −.25), and effect of weak local Democratic party organizations (*beta* .39). From this point on, differences may be noted.

I had earlier assumed that salaries and committee chair assignments might prove to be important incentives to seek a legislative post. If so, women might find entering these legislative chambers most difficult, and it would seem to be true in the North. States where legislative salaries are significantly greater than the prevailing median per capita income, are

TABLE 2.4
Multiple Regression Analyses' *Betas* of Women's Northern Representation in Three Elections

Independent Variables	All Women*	Democrats	Republicans
Females Employed	.57 a	.49 a	.62 a
Educ. 16 Years +	−.41 b	−.41 b	−.39 b
Local Democratic Orgns.	.39 c	.41 c	.35 c
Metropolitan Pop.	.36 c	.37 c	.34 c
Legislative Salary	−.35 c	−.35 c	−.33 c
Committee Chairs	−.25 c	−.28 c	−.32 c
Antidiscrimination	−.25 c	−.28 c	−.20 d
Black Population	.34 c	.22 NS	.44 c
Roman Catholic	−.25 d	−.25 d	−.24 d
Chamber to Democrats	−.16 NS	−.10 NS	−.21 c
R square	.47	.47	.48

Notes:
Reports only those *betas* that are significant for one or all groups of women.
a = T-test sig. < .001; b = T-test sig. < .01; c = T-test sig. < .05; d = T-test sig. < .10; NS = not significant.
*All women except blacks and Hispanics.

likely to be a barrier to women's representation (*beta* −.35). In addition, those states with more committee chairs as a proportion of the total membership also seem to be difficult barriers to women's political ambition. When one assesses this in the context of northern states, I must again raise some questions about the likely ambiguity of metropolitan characteristics. Generally, large metropolitan states like New York, California, Illinois, and Pennsylvania have considerable salaries, although states like Wisconsin and Minnesota also pay their legislators very well.

The exclusion of the South's conservative Protestants has the notable effect of decreasing its significance to predict women's representation (*beta* −.11). Nor does Roman Catholicism (*beta* −.25), although it does indicate a marginal (significant < .10) barrier to women's representation. Finally, in this subsample, the proportion of the black population represents a positive, but marginal, predictor of their representation (*beta* .34). This indicates, at least, that women are doing well in metropolitan states where the black population is likely to be found.

Northern Variations — Partisan Differences

The variance explained by the multiple regression analyses of Democratic and Republican females is 47 percent and 48 percent, respectively. The explanation of variance is similar to the analyses of all females in the North, but it is somewhat greater than the national analyses. Much like the assessment of national variations, a number of variables seem equally important in predicting Democratic women's political success in state legislatures. However, there is one subtle difference. At least in the North, the number of women employed in the economy (*beta* .49) seems to be the best of six significant independent variables. In essence, the impact of the rights revolution and inflationary spiral of the 1970s has drawn women into the marketplace thereby increasing their political consciousness. This in turn has meant more women have sought political office as they entered appropriate professions associated with eligibility pools.[20] The proportion of the population that is well educated still does not predict women's representation (*beta* −.41). This represents a difficult, ambiguous finding. I would think that northern metropolitan states (which also predict Democratic female representation: *beta* .37) would be states with high proportions of such well-educated citizens. Democrats in the North traditionally represent metropolitan areas, but for Democratic women, that representation is likely to occur where the local Democratic party organizations are relatively weak (*beta* .41).

It is this contradiction between metropolitan characteristics and weak Democratic party organizations that is difficult to interpret. As a rule, strong Democratic organizations exist in metropolitan states. If one assesses Elazar's individualistic political culture and probes Mayhew's introduction to traditional party organization states, one finds that the independent variables associated with each have little impact on women's representation.[21] In addition, Roman Catholicism is a marginally significant (*beta* −.25) barrier to Democratic women's political success. Customarily, large Roman Catholic, ethnic populations are found in metropolitan states with strong local party organizations. I believe this is further evidence that Democratic females, at least during the conservative 1980s, are having difficulty obtaining support from traditional Democratic groups.

A differentiation of women on the basis of partisan attachments and regional differences over time increases our understanding of the incentives found in legislative office. Legislative salaries were assumed to be important incentives in explaining why individuals might seek political office. As Squire indicates, salaries and positions within the legislature are likely to affect membership stability, and the inverse relationship (*beta* −.35) between salaries and Democratic women's representation may to some extent underscore the impact of incumbency and the stagnation of women's representation during this period.[22] However, the assessment of national variation indicates that women tend to do better when there is no change, particularly in party control. Although not significant by any means, an inverse relationship (*beta* −.16) between a change to Democratic control with Democratic women's representation is worth pondering. Perhaps there is some truth that where salaries are greater and the number of leadership positions (committees *beta* −.27 is marginally significant) greater, women are not likely to be greatly represented.

If anything, this inquiry also finds that a longer history of antidiscrimination laws (*beta* −.28) seems to be one very positive facilitator of Democratic women's representation. Although it proves to be insignificant for Republican women, the historical emphasis on equality in legislation seems quite important in the North for all women and especially Democratic women. Conditionally, we may infer that the greater barriers to Democratic women within traditional Democratic constituencies are substantially softened by existing antidiscrimination statutes. Republican women do not face the same political barriers within their traditional constituencies.

The state characteristics that predict Republican success are similar yet subtly different. As in the study of national variations, the major predictor of Republican representation is the proportion of females who are in the marketplace (*beta* .62). Similarly, the regression analysis indicates that the state populations will not have a large percentage of their citizens with 16 or more years of education (*beta* −.39). The remaining independent variables reflect some likely relationships with political parties. If there are weak, local Democratic party organizations, Republican women have better success (*beta* .35) as do their female counterparts across the aisle. This difference between Democrats and Republicans may indicate that Democrats must be self-starters running their own campaign organizations whereas Republicans might obtain support from their party. However, this seems unlikely because local Republican organizations have little, if any, predictive capacity for female representation. Surprisingly, a change to Democratic control does have ironic consequences. Republican women are likely to do better where no change occurs (*beta* −.21), and their representation is likely to be less, or decline, if their party loses control of a chamber. If true, can one infer that in political turmoil and uncertainty, the loss of seats is likely to affect Republican females more than males? If so, this would provide further evidence that in more competitive situations males are likely to retain seats.

Much like Democratic women, Republican representation is likely to occur in legislatures whose salaries as a proportion of the median per capita income is smaller (*beta* −.33). Similarly, the *beta* (−.32) for the number of committee chairs as a proportion of total chamber membership is likely to be smaller. In this respect, the findings are similar to Rule's and at odds with findings reported by R. Darcy et al.[23]

Finally, the metropolitan attributes of the U.S. states significantly predict women's representation (*beta* .34). Not merely the metropolitan characteristics, but the larger the proportion of blacks, the greater the female Republican representation (*beta* .44). This finding reverses the analysis of national variations. I do not for a moment think that the black metropolitan population in northern states will electorally support women who themselves are not black, but if we are to use state characteristics to assess women's political success, we must do so with extreme caution.

There is only one marginal independent variable of note, Roman Catholicism (*beta* −.23). In one sense this is politically predictable for Republican females because Roman Catholic ethnics have traditionally voted Democratic. Yet, the variable also represents a marginal barrier affecting women in the Democratic Party. It would appear one could conclude that a pervasive bias against women and party attachment have some impact on Republican females in the North.

Southern Variations — All Women

The variations associated with the South are likely to be different for a number of reasons. First, the number of cases (30) during this time period creates problems for any analysis. Second, women's representation, and especially Republican representation, is quite small when compared to the North. For these reasons, the findings should be accepted with great caution. It is highly likely that any finding could be a random response to unusual events of the 1980s.

The multiple regression analysis of all women's representation explains about 60 percent of the variance, and only two variables significantly predict their political success: traditional party organizations and the proportion of the population that is conservative Protestants (see Table 2.5). Although a traditional party organization state is unique in the South, a woman is less likely to achieve legislative office in this environment (*beta* –1.13). I can only believe that this finding, surprising as it is, is probably far fetched because Louisiana, tagged by Mayhew as a traditional party organization, is not included in the analysis.[24] Perhaps more important is the impact of conservative Protestants (*beta* –.103), who represent a very important barrier to women's representation. I think that this independent variable is more viable given my earlier national results. The conclusion one can make is that as the proportion of Protestants declines, barriers to women's representation are also likely to decrease.

Two remaining independent variables are marginal, but they do reflect earlier results. The proportion of the population with 16 years of education, or more, has an inverse (*beta* –1.01) relationship with women's representation. Again, this is a surprising finding if one thinks that higher educational levels should increase tolerance. As expected, women's representation is marginally and inversely related to the proportion of the population that is black. As reported above, this is politically expected because legislators often manifest the racial, religious, and ethnic attributes of their constituents.

Southern Variations — Partisan Differences

When one differentiates women by partisan attachment in the South, the dependent variable's variation in percentage values sharply decreases. This is particularly true of Republican female representation, and the regression analysis explains 51 percent of the variance compared to 75 percent of the variance in the Democratic regression analysis.

TABLE 2.5

Multiple Regression Analyses' *Betas* **of Women's Southern Representation in Chambers in Three Elections**

Independent Variables	All Women*	Democrats	Republicans
Tradition Party Orgn.	−1.13 b	.50 NS	−1.11 c
Cons. Protestants	−1.03 b	−1.22 b	−.09 NS
Educ. 16 Years +	−1.01 d	−.83 d	−.53 NS
Black Population	−.62 d	−.17 NS	−.73 c
Hispanic Population	−.36 NS	−.36 d	−.11 NS
Democratic Orgns.	—	.36 d	−.11 NS
Committee Chairs	.64 NS	.77 d	.04 NS
R square	.60	.75	.51

Notes:

Reports only those *betas* that are significant for one or all groups of women in this analysis.

b = T-test sig. < .01; c = T-test sig. < .05; d = T-test sig. < .10; NS = not significant.

*All women except blacks and Hispanics.

My analysis of Democratic females indicates that only one of the independent variables significantly predicts their representation: conservative Protestantism. It remains a difficult barrier to women's representation rooted in religious values. It is little wonder that women's political success is so meager in this region.

Other than the pervasive religious bias directed at women, four marginally significant variables indicate that Democratic women are likely to succeed in states with less than 16 years of education (*beta* −.83). This finding is much like that found in the North and national analyses, and again unexpected. Second, Democrats are likely to do better where the number of committee chairs as a proportion of the total membership is likely to be greater (*beta* .77). Does this suggest a lack of professionalism within these states or a greater incentive to obtain office? Because this finding contradicts earlier analyses, it is, at best, difficult to affix a precise interpretation. Finally, Democratic women seem to do better when a local Democratic party is a less viable organization (*beta* .36) and when the proportion of the Hispanic population is negligible (*beta* −.36). Local Democratic organizations have been found to be weak in the North and nationally where Democratic women have had political success. The fewer the number of Hispanics, the greater may non-Hispanic women's representation be politically expected. Constituents are likely to choose legislators who are more like themselves. Each of these predictors either complements earlier analyses or is logically expected.

Republican representation is significantly explained by two independent variables: traditional party organizations and the proportion of the population that is black. Each of these variables represents a logical outcome if I were not so cautious about the number of cases and small variation found in my southern dependent variables. Republican women may be expected not to do well in traditional party organization states (*beta* –1.11), which are likely to be overwhelmingly Democratic. In this sense, Republican success is somewhat similar to the success of Democratic women, which is likely to occur where a local Democratic party is not particularly strong. To this, the expected inverse (*beta* –.73) relationship with the size of a black population represents a historical pattern in which constituents vote for legislators with similar characteristics. Of course, it should be noted that the black population votes eight and nine to one for Democratic candidates. No other independent variables even marginally predict the admittedly meager Republican success in the South.

The above analysis of women's representation indicates some new, significant findings. I believe the research has always assumed that women's representation is greater if more women are employed in the economic work force. In addition, it indicates that women also do well in states with metropolitan attributes, at least in an analysis of national and northern samples. The South is different, but I think this may be due in some small part to the minute variation that exists in women's representation, particularly Republican, from state to state. One attribute of these states is the proportion of the population with 16 years of education, or more, in which women's representation is less likely to be found. This is unexpected because I reasoned that states with a higher proportion of well-educated citizens ought to have more tolerant citizens.

I think that the most unique findings are those associated with Democratic and Republican women's representation and with the effect of conservative religious sects, Protestant and Roman Catholic. In the national sample, both represent important barriers to women's representation — whether Republican or Democratic. Roman Catholicism is marginally important in the North for all groups in this analysis, and in the South, conservative Protestants have a significant impact on all women and on Democrats, but not on Republicans. Perhaps this is the reason Republican female success is growing in the South and Democratic success is declining during this three-election-year period. Finally, legislative salaries as a proportion of per capita median income in the states is a predictor of women's representation. Other studies that indicated legislative salaries were not significant did not differentiate between regions and partisan attachments. For Democratic women nationally, their representation occurs where the difference between legislative salary and per capita income is smaller; hence, there are fewer incentives to seek political office for economic reasons. This might indicate that earlier studies are probably correct to assume that legislative salaries may create incentives to enter the legislature. If so, women did poorly in the 1970s. In the North, a similar relationship exists for all women, Democratic women, and Republican women. Women do better where the potential economic incentives are not as great.

A number of independent variables do not predict female legislative success, and these are quite important. Metropolitan populations predict women's political success, and in doing so, states with multimember district plans do not as indicated in earlier studies. The assumptions have been made that women were less competitive and did better in multi-member districts where there was less competition. Earlier studies have historically indicated that women were unlikely to do well in metropolitan areas with large legislative districts until the 1980s, the period associated with this study. The glacial advance of women's representation during this period may be an interlude in which women come to grips with their new heterogeneous constituencies, and these constituents must in turn learn to accept female politicians. In addition, contrary to expectations, changes related to party control indicate no positive, significant relationship with women's representation. If changes in party control cause some incumbents to retire or be defeated at the polls, women have not benefited by increasing their numbers as a proportion of full chamber membership. In fact, the insignificant *beta* weights are negative. This may suggest that in this very competitive environment, others do well.

National Variations — Blacks and Hispanics

A preliminary examination of black and Hispanic representation must be quick to point out that differences between these groups is not merely ethnic or racial. Their partisan attachments are quite different. Generally, blacks are Democrats (although there is one black Republican legislator in Alaska). That much is clear, but the heterogeneity of the Hispanic (Spanish-speaking) population is reflected in different partisan attachments. There are three major streams of Hispanics: Puerto Ricans, Cubans, and Mexican-Americans. Puerto Ricans, found in New York, tend to be Democrats. Since the 1970s, the Puerto Rican community has become more active in politics, either by using existing local Democratic organizations to advance their interests or by building independent power bases. Although there has been increased activism, Puerto Ricans in 1984 had the lowest registration rate in New York City.[25] The Cuban population, found in Florida and New York, is generally conservative, anti-Communist, and most likely to vote Republican. They differ from Puerto Ricans in that a larger percentage of the earlier immigrants were better educated and skilled and, therefore, more likely to be registered and vote.[26]

Mexican-Americans were the earliest and most recent immigrants to the United States. They are often found in major metropolitan states in segregated communities in New York, Illinois, California, Florida, and Texas. They also represent a good proportion of the population found in New Mexico, Arizona, and Colorado. It is highly likely that they will represent the largest ethnic group in southern California in the last decade of this millennium.[27] Although Mexican-American registration is low (35 percent in 1984), increased political activism will probably occur within the Democratic Party in the coming decades.

These few facts lend credence to the efficacy of differentiating these groups in terms of the partisan attachments. In doing so, one must remember that there are few legislators in the United States and therefore treat the multiple regression analyses with some caution. First, I will assess black representation in the nation followed by an evaluation of Hispanic political success.

The regression analysis of black representation explains 41 percent of the variance, and three closely grouped, independent variables are very significant: percent of the population with 16 or more years of education, percent of the females employed in the states, and percent of the population living in metropolitan areas (Table 2.6). If there is a surprise in this analysis, it is the insignificant impact of the percent of the population that is black to predict black representation. It is significant when one differentiates between the regions, but not in this national analysis. However this may be, there are some similarities to the regression analyses of Democratic females. Although one would not expect that the proportion of the population with at least 16 years of education would be inversely related to Democratic women, one might expect it to inversely (*beta* −.55) predict black representation. The black population is generally less educated, and the attribute should predict black representation. Like Democratic females, the percent of females employed (*beta* .50) and the importance of the antidiscrimination index (*beta* −.30) are important predictors of black political success. Black

TABLE 2.6
Multiple Regression Analyses' *Betas* **of Black and**
Hispanic National Representation in Chambers in
Three Elections

	Black	*Hispanics*		
Independent Variables	*Dems.*	*All*	*Dems.*	*Reps.*
Educ. 16 Years +	−.55 a	−.48 a	−.46 a	−.49 a
Females Employed	.50 a	.43 a	.40 a	.44 b
Metropolitan Pop.	.48 a	.38 b	.33 b	.42 b
Roman Catholics	−.35 b	−.35 b	−.32 b	−.36 b
Antidiscrimination	−.30 c	−.29 c	−.29 c	−.28 c
Democratic Orgns.	.25 c	.25 d	.26 c	.22 d
Cons. Protestants	−.23 c	−.24 c	−.21 d	−.27 c
Hispanic Pop.	.14 NS	.28 c	.45 a	.10 NS
Legis. Salary	.10 NS	−.19 NS	−.17 NS	−.21 d
R square	.41	.38	.44	.35

Notes:
Reports only those *betas* that are significant for one or all of the minority groups.
a = T-test sig. < .001; b = T-test sig. < .01; c = T-test sig. < .05; d = T-test sig.
< .10; NS = not significant.

advancement during the "rights revolution" of the 1950s through the 1970s parallels female advancement. The broad range of antidiscrimination statutes that lowered barriers for women also lowered barriers for blacks. In fact, more precisely, antidiscrimination statutes directed at racial discrimination probably had "spillover" effects for women in society. Although not directly measured here, the employment of women due to changes in legal and cultural values probably affects black employment opportunities as well.

Not surprising, a major positive predictor of black political advancement in state legislatures is the percent of the population living in metropolitan areas (*beta* .48). This is expected because an extremely large percentage of blacks live in large metropolitan centers: 60 percent in 1970 and 57.8 percent in 1980.[28] Much like Democratic females, black representation is most probable where the percentage of Protestants (*beta* −.23) and Roman Catholics (*beta* −.35) is likely to be small. These inverse relationships reinforce Peek and Brown's earlier research that the pervasive biblical bias against women found in these religious sects also includes some racial discrimination (e.g., the biblical story of the behavior of Noah's black son).[29] I think one may explain the racial discrimination due in part to factors outside specific religious values. It may have more to do with the political conflict with Roman Catholic, ethnic, machine Democrats in northern metropolitan states and tentatively white conservative Protestants in the South. This alternative explanation is strengthened by the positive, predictive capacity of local Democratic organizations (*beta* .25). This positive relationship indicates less efficacious, local Democratic organizations favor black representation (much like, again, Democratic females). If the Democratic Party's local organizations are more effective, then blacks, like women and Hispanics, will find their road to political success in lower state legislative chambers more difficult.

The multiple regression analyses of Hispanic political success and those differentiated by partisan attachment explain 38 percent (all Hispanics), 44 percent (Democrats), and 35 (Republican) percent of the variance (Table 2.6). Hispanic representation is predicted by similar variables that significantly predicted black and female representation. Two very important factors are the percentage of the population with 16 years of education or more and percent of females employed in each state. It would not be surprising to find that the education independent variable had a significant, inverse relationship (*beta* −.48 for all Hispanics) with Hispanic political success (*betas* −.46 for Democrats and −.49 for Republicans). One would not expect a large percentage of new immigrants from a different cultural tradition to have completed a university education, much less an advanced degree. Much like blacks and females, the percent of females employed is also a significant, positive (*beta* .43) predictor of Hispanic representation, a pattern that is also shared by Democratic and Republican Hispanics (*betas:* .40 and .44 respectively).

I think, and this is a restatement of earlier analyses, that this is due in part to the significant impact of the antidiscrimination index for all three Hispanic groups (*betas:* all Hispanics, −.29; Democrats, −.29; Republicans, −.28). Antidiscrimination statutes and women's employment seem to reflect environments that have opened avenues into politics. To these variables, states with metropolitan attributes also predict where Hispanics are likely to do well (*betas*: all Hispanics, .38; Democratic, .33; Republican, .42). Approximately 65 percent of the Hispanic population resides in either New York, Illinois, Florida, Texas, or California, and nearly 50 percent lives in central cities.[30]

From this point on, the analyses must be read cautiously as one might read the tea leaves of future history. One might expect that conservative

Protestants would represent an inverse relationship with Hispanic representation (*betas*: all Hispanics, −.24; Democrats marginally significant < .10, −.21; Republicans, −.27). After all, the racial, ethnic, and religious attributes of voters are often mirrored in the legislators they elect. However, the significant, inverse relationship with the proportion of a state population that is Roman Catholic (*betas*: all Hispanics, −.35; Democrats, −.32; Republicans, −.36) is anomalous and reflects, in this case, a crucial weakness in using statewide religious attributes to explain group representation. Because the percentage of the population that is Hispanic significantly predicts all Hispanic representation (*beta* .28) and Democratic success (*beta* .45), caution is essential. This may signify that the Hispanic population was not accurately counted in the 1980 census, and one might expect that the 1980 report on religious affiliation is also likely to be inaccurate. Of course, there may be another reason for this relationship.

Much like Democratic black and female politicians, it seems that all Hispanics do better if the local Democratic party is not particularly well organized. Perhaps this variable, tied to existing strong parties associated with other ethnic Roman Catholics, indicates the reasons for a negative relationship with Roman Catholicism. James Shortridge differentiates Roman Catholics by indicating that French and Hispanic populations are "super Catholics" in the practice of their religion, but this difference was not noted in my source materials.[31]

Northern Variations — Blacks and Hispanics

Approximately 49 percent of the variance of black representation is explained in the analysis of northern states (see Table 2.7). Although many of the national predictors remain significant in this region, some differences enhance our understanding of black political success. The proportion of the population with 16 years of education or more remains a significant, inverse predictor (*beta* −.52) of success in lower state legislative chambers. This relationship might be expected given the relative poverty and educational achievement in the black community, particularly in the large, northern, metropolitan (*beta* .42) states with large black populations (*beta* .54). This latter independent variable, percent of the population that is black, is expected but was not a significant predictor in the national analysis. Although this is an additional, but expected relationship, the percent of females employed (*beta* .51) and the state antidiscrimination index (*beta* −.24) manifest significant impact on black representation. There has always been a

TABLE 2.7
Multiple Regression Analyses' *Betas* **of Black and Hispanic Northern Representation in Chambers in Three Elections**

Independent Variables	Black Dems.	Hispanics		
		All	Dems.	Reps.
Educ. 16 Years +	−.52 a	−.46 a	−.46 a	−.47 a
Females Employed	.51 a	.45 a	.42 a	.47 a
Black Population	.54 b	.37 d	.36 d	.38 d
Metropolitan Pop.	.42 b	.35 c	.33 c	.37 c
Democratic Orgns.	.33 c	.29 d	.26 d	.30 d
Legis. Salary	−.30 c	−.37 c	−.33 c	−.40 c
Committee Chairs	−.30 c	−.27 c	−.26 c	−.27 d
Antidiscrimination	−.24 c	−.22 d	−.21 d	−.23 d
Roman Catholics	−.21 d	−.21 NS	−.20 NS	−.21 NS
Hispanic Pop.	.17 NS	.32 c	.49 b	.13 NS
R square	.49	.43	.50	.43

Notes:
Reports only those *betas* that are significant for one or more of the minority groups.

a = T-test sig. < .001; b = T-test sig. < .01; c = T-test sig. < .05; d = T-test sig. < .10; NS = not significant.

tendency in the North to assume that segregation in the South, particularly *de jure* segregation, was a regional phenomenon. However, one may assume that *de facto* segregation, and an uneven development of antidiscrimination statutes in the North, is an explanation for black political success as well. The impact of these statutes may be tied in part to the percent of females employed in the state, an analysis found above in the discussion of female success and black national representation.

Other barriers to black ambition are also implicit. The role of local Democratic organizations is what one might expect. One might assume that well-organized, local Democratic organizations dominated by ethnics are likely to be significant barriers (*beta* .33) to black representation. This analysis is enhanced by the marginal, inverse (*beta* −.21, significant < .10), relationship with the percent of Roman Catholics who have been central city mainstays to local Democratic parties. In part, this represents the political conflict within metropolitan areas between white, Roman Catholic, ethnic Democrats and blacks. This conflict is nationally manifested in the strain between the Reverend Jesse Jackson's liberalism and Governor Michael Dukakis's centrism to obtain white support in the 1988 presidential election.

Given the nature of poor black communities, one would expect that legislative salaries and the number of committee chairs might be important concerns for social advancement. They do, but the relationships are unexpected, particularly for legislative salaries (*beta* −.30). This means that there is a small difference between legislative salaries and state median per capita income (e.g., legislative salaries/median per capita income). The finding is similar to females in the North, but it does raise a question of interpretive ambiguity in correlational analysis using state attributes. Most blacks live in central cities, and the median per capita incomes within black wards are likely to be below the state median. As with females, we must ask, "Which metropolitan population underlies this analysis?" The number of committee chairs as a proportion of total chamber membership (*beta* −.30) indicates fewer chairs for majority party members. I had assumed a positive relationship because an increased number of chairs wold increase the likelihood of real policy achievements in the legislative process. One does not simply become one of 99 or 200 legislators, one becomes one of a small number of influentials who have some real control of the legislature's policy agenda.[32]

Hispanic representation yields greater percentages of variance explained than those based on a national sample: 43 percent for all Hispanics, 50 percent for Democrats, and 43 percent for Republicans (Table 2.7). The independent variables that predict Hispanic representation are quite similar to explanations of black (and earlier female) represen-tation with some differences (especially the percent of the population that is Hispanic).

Much like the independent variables predicting black and female representation in the North, state attributes concerning the percent of the population with 16 or more years of education (*betas*: all Hispanics, −.46; Democrats, −.46; Republicans, −.47) and percent females employed (*betas*: all Hispanics, .45; Democrats, .42; Republicans .47) explain a good part of Hispanic representation. An inverse relationship between the education independent variable is not unexpected. The Hispanic communities in the United States are highly unlikely to have a high proportion of college-educated citizens. The percent of females employed seems to indicate states that have avenues for social mobility, although the existence of antidiscrimination statutes is only marginally (significance < .10) related to Hispanic representation (*betas*: all Hispanics, −.22; Democrats, −.21; Republicans, −.23).

As expected, Hispanic representation in the North is found in large metropolitan states (*betas*: all Hispanics, .35; Democrats, .33; Republicans, .37) and where there is a large percentage of blacks (*betas*: all Hispanics, .37; Democrats, .36; Republicans, .38; all these are marginally significant < .10). With the exception of Republican Hispanics (whose percentage of state legislative chambers is smaller), the size of a state's Hispanic population significantly predicts Hispanic political success (*betas*: all Hispanics, .32; Democrats, .49; Republicans, .13, not significant). These relationships suggest the possibility of political conflict in metropolitan areas between emerging Hispanic strength and existing black representation in state and local offices. As Hispanics register to vote and begin to participate in large numbers, they are likely to displace either, or both, of two groups: other Roman Catholic ethnics from Europe or blacks. One may infer this from the above and following relationships.

It is clear that Hispanics do not do well where local Democratic organizations are strong. Their political success has occurred where the local Democratic parties are quite weak (*betas*: all Hispanics, .29; Democrats, .26; Republicans, .30). The size of the Roman Catholic population does not even marginally predict Hispanic success, but one should note that an inverse relationship is evident (see Table 2.7). It would appear that Hispanics probably represent a minority of Roman Catholics in these northern states, and perhaps they are not precisely counted by the Roman Catholic Church.

These findings strengthen my suspicions in reading the tea leaves of future political history. One scenario might have European Roman Catholic Democratic organizations seeking a coalition with increasingly active Hispanics to offset black political power. Although I have no clear evidence of this, it seems that Chicago Mayor Richard Daley, Jr., may have sought to do just that in his successful bid for office. Of course, it is feasible that political cooperation may occur between some Hispanic groups and blacks (Puerto Ricans and blacks in the New York legislature). It is apparent that issues of race and religion will play an important role in explaining coalition behavior in metropolitan states, for example, Puerto Ricans acting in concert with blacks and Mexican-Hispanics with Roman Catholic Europeans. Whatever happens, one must remember that central city populations have been declining, therefore sharper political competition is likely to occur between these groups. This is particularly true in the Northeast and Midwest, which will probably lose U.S. Congressional seats to the South and Southwest. In addition, in the forthcoming reapportionment of the 1990s, central city representation may also decline in state legislatures.

Finally, legislative salary (*betas*: all Hispanics, −.37; Democrats, −.33; Republicans, −.40) and committee chair (*betas*: all Hispanics, −.27; Democrats, −.26; Republicans, −.27, < .10) indices act much like those predicting black representation. Hispanics do better politically where there are likely to be fewer incentives for legislative office and fewer chairs to be shared by the majority party. Of course, if we were to assess representation within districts, would we find that low per capita incomes and high legislative salaries found in many metropolitan states might provide significant, positive predictors of their political success? I believe so. For this reason, the correlational analysis yields interpretive ambiguity, and once again caution is advised.

Southern Variations — Black and Hispanic

The South is different, and this is most evident by the unusually large explanation of 96 percent of variance associated with black representation (Table 2.8). Unlike the analysis of Northern black representation, the relationship between most of the significant independent variables "behave" as one would expect in a more ideal setting. Perhaps the most surprising finding is the positive effect of multimember districts (*beta* 1.36), a variable that was to predict women's representation positively, but did not. Contemporary evidence indicates that multimember districts are likely to favor women candidates to the detriment of other minorities.[33] Although this analysis does not differentiate between black males and females, the next chapter, comparing gender success for blacks and Hispanics as a percent of their representation in their respective parties, indicates that multimember districts in the South are more important for black males than females.

The second most important state attribute predicting black political success was the number of standing committee chairs as a proportion of chamber members. I had thought that a greater proportion of chairs would be an incentive to enter legislative politics. Since most legislative chambers, and certainly all chambers in the South, are Democratic, one would think that minimally the proportion of committee chairs would be an important incentive to Democrats. However, one cannot make a case for incentives based on the availability of chairs because an inverse relationship (*beta* −1.06) exists. In fact, when this variable has significantly predicted minority representation, it has always been a

TABLE 2.8
Multiple Regression Analyses' *Betas* of Black and
Hispanic Southern Representation in Chambers in
Three Elections

Independent Variables	Black Dems.	Hispanics All	Hispanics Dems.	Hispanics Reps.
Multimember Dist.	1.36 a	−.36 NS	.03 NS	−1.01 c
Committee Chairs	−1.06 a	.26 NS	−.02 NS	.72 b
Educ. 16 Years +	.90 b	−.42 d	−.02 NS	−1.06 a
Cons. Protestants	.86 a	−.27 NS	.15 NS	−1.08 a
Black Population	.84 a	−.09 NS	−.19 NS	.24 NS
Republican Orgns.	.55 a	−.08 NS	−.19 NS	.25 NS
Democratic Orgns.	−.55 a	.11 NS	.31 b	−.48 a
Hispanic Pop.	.52 a	.91 a	.87 a	.23 d
Trad. Party Orgns.	.52 a	−.31 d	−.15 NS	−.43 c
R square	.92	.94	.95	.91

Notes:
Reports only those *betas* that are significant with one or more of the minorities.
a = T-test sig. < .001; b = T-test sig. < .01; c = T-test sig. < .05; d = T-test sig. < .10; NS = not significant.

negative. Seemingly, we might assume that the legislative chambers with fewer chairs imply tightly knit committee systems with little overlapping policy specialization. These attributes may indicate greater professionalism, accountability, and, perhaps, progressiveness. If this does suggest greater progressiveness in modernizing state institutions, then this atmosphere has also affected other political decisions — like voting.

Progressive action is likely to occur among better educated populations, and educational attainment is associated with greater tolerance. For that reason, one would expect that a greater percentage of people with a college degree (and more) would positively predict minority representation. In the North, the opposite is true; in the South, this educational attribute positively (*beta* .90) predicts black representation. In addition, the proportion of conservative Protestants also positively predicts black success. Although Bernard Quinn et al. do not include the membership of black churches in the United States, one might assume that black

Protestant churches would parallel the existence of white Protestant churches in the South.[34] This is the likely interpretation one may ascribe to this relationship. This interpretation is strengthened by the expected positive effect of the percentage of blacks in a state (*beta* .84). This is at variance with earlier analyses in which white, fundamentalist Protestantism represented an inverse relationship with black success in the analysis of national representation.

Political party organizations in the South represent a neat, predictable relationship with black representation. Assuming parties are involved in recruitment and the mobilization of voters, blacks who are eight and nine to one Democratic, should find positive support from local Democratic organizations. In fact, in areas where there are large percentages of black voters, blacks may have taken over local Democratic organizations. Or given the rise of Republican organizations, blacks are necessary to a successful Democratic coalition. Either explanation, or both, is likely because local Democratic organizations represent an inverse (*beta* −.55) relationship with black success. (Remember the independent variable is rank ordered from more effective to less effective local party organizations.) Local Republican organizations are likely to be weaker and should, in fact do, represent a positive (*beta* .55) relationship with black legislative success.

Finally, black representation is also found in states where there are large percentages of Hispanics (*beta* .52). These Hispanics are likely to be found in Florida and Texas and, as such, represent Republican and Democratic activists, respectively, in the South. Again, this implies that potential political conflict does and will exist between blacks and Hispanics over the allocation of goods and services. In Florida, it will be largely partisan conflict; in Texas, it may come to represent intraparty factionalism. As more Mexican-Americans register and become politically active, this conflict will probably intensify. If these Texas Democrats do not fight among themselves, they may act in concert against white party organizational activists who may drift further (or be driven) into the arms of the Republican Party. Clearly, the politics of the next few decades will become more intriguing as Hispanics enter mainstream political organizations (or take them over).

My regression analyses of Hispanic representation explain 97, 97, and 95 percent of the variance for all Hispanics, Democrats, and Republicans respectively (Table 2.8). The analytical strategy for differentiating minority groups by party attachments becomes quite apparent. A good number of differences appear in the attributes that predict Democratic and Republican Hispanic legislative success. However, a cautionary note is essential. I am not confident of these findings because there are so few Hispanics in southern state legislatures.

If one were to assess southern Hispanic success as a single group, blurring partisan attachments, only one significant predictor of their representation would be found: percent of the population that is Hispanic (*beta* .91). That is entirely predictable, and two marginally significant variables predict their success. The most important of these indicates that Hispanic representation is likely to occur in states where the percent of the population with 16 years of education, or more, was not very great (*beta* −.42). This provides a different finding from the one associated with black success, but it might be expected assuming that not many Hispanics are likely to be well educated. Neither local party organization seems important, but there is a negative, marginally significant relationship between traditional party organization states (*beta* −.31) and Hispanic representation. Again, it is unlikely there are any significant numbers of Mexican-Americans, Puerto Ricans, or Cuban-Americans in, for example, West Virginia. In this sense, one cannot interpret that traditional party organization states are barriers to Hispanic representation if there are no significant numbers of Hispanics in those states.

There is a paucity of solid data to predict Democratic Hispanic success. Again, the percentage of the population remains the most significant predictor (*beta* .87) of their legislative success. They also seem to have better success if their own political party is relatively ineffective (*beta* .31). This is quite different from the explanation of black representation where a strong local Democratic party was an important facilitator. This seems to suggest that Democratic Hispanics will do better where white or black dominated, local party organizations are weak. They are specifically weak where there are large numbers of Hispanics, which suggests that Hispanics have not yet organized effectively for political success.

The explanation of Republican success is far more extensive. Seven significant and marginal independent variables are important in explaining Republican Hispanic success, and a marginal predictor is the percentage of Hispanics in a state (*beta* .23). This alone is surprising. It might be explained by the predictive capacities of local Democratic organizations. Republican Hispanics seem to be doing well where the local Democratic party is highly effective (*beta* −.48). This may mean that their recruitment is enhanced within the Republican party to offset Democratic strength, especially in Florida. Traditional party organization states are also inversely (*beta* −.43) related to their success indicating that state party organizations are generally weak.

Republican Hispanic success is likely to be found in states whose attributes are very different from those which predict black success: multimember districts, committee chair index, education, and the percentage of conservative Protestants in states. In fact, all the relationships are in an opposite direction from those that predict black Democratic representation. As might be expected, there is a strong, inverse relationship (*beta* −1.08) between the conservative Protestant population and Roman Catholic Hispanics. The population of the states with Hispanic representation will probably have a smaller proportion of citizens with 16 or more years of education (*beta* −1.06) and not have multimember district plans (*beta* −1.01). These states will also have a larger proportion of standing committee chairs (*beta* .72) as a percent of chamber membership.

The richness of this analysis that differentiates minorities by party attachment is clearly superior to those analyses that simply assess a group. Those studies that do not do so are more realistically attached to the symbolic meaning of each group's entry into the political mainstream. But, as one will note, regression analyses of groups do, in fact, gloss over important attributes that predict partisan success within each group.

Perhaps the most important aspects in this study of representation are the importance of religion and their implications for female, black, and Hispanic representation. Although one might expect an inverse relationship between Roman Catholicism and female Republican success, given the traditional Roman Catholic ethnic opposition to Republicans, what are the implications when there is also an inverse relationship with female Democrats? The traditional support for Democrats is found in northern metropolitan states with Roman Catholic ethnics. What implications are there for female Democrats whose representation also reflects an inverse relationship with conservative Protestants, particularly when white Southerners traditionally support Democratic candidates in state and local elections? Can we say in this period of conservatism that issues such as abortion and a pervasive biblical bias against women in these conservative religious sects have slowed female political ambitions? These findings coupled with other significant predictors tell us a good deal more about female, black, and Hispanic political success. The analysis has a richer content that expresses more of the cultural values that serve to inhibit or facilitate minority incorporation.

NOTES

1. John F. Bibby, "Pattern of Midterm Gubernatorial and State Legislative Elections," *Public Opinion Quarterly* 6 (1983): 41–46; James E. Campbell,

"Presidential Coattails and Midterm Loses in State Legislative Elections," *American Political Science Review* 80 (March 1986): 45–64.

2. Bibby, ibid.; Campbell, ibid.

3. Michael S. Lewis-Beck, *Applied Regression* (Beverly Hills: Sage, 1980), p. 65.

4. Kristi Anderson, "Working Women and Political Participation, 1952–1972," *American Journal of Political Science* 19 (August 1975): 439–53. Also see Robert A. Dahl, *After the Revolution?* (New Haven: Yale University Press, 1970); Carole Pateman, *Participation and Democratic Theory* (Cambridge: Cambridge University Press, 1970); William H. Flanigan and Nancy H. Zingale, *Political Behavior and the American Electorate* (Boston: Allyn and Bacon, 1987).

5. R. Darcy, Susan Welch, and Janet Clark, *Women, Elections, and Representation* (New York: Longman, 1987).

6. Wilma Rule, "Why Women Don't Run," *Western Political Quarterly* 34 (March 1984): 60–77; Darcy et al., *Women, Elections, and Representation.*

7. Carol Nechemias, "Geographic Mobility and Women's Access to State Legislatures," *Western Political Quarterly* 38 (March 1985): 119–31.

8. See Irene Diamond, *Sex Roles in the State House* (New Haven: Yale University Press, 1977); Daniel J. Elazar, *American Federalism: A View from the States* (New York: Thomas Y. Crowell, 1972); Albert J. Nelson, "Political Culture and Women's Representation in Lower State Legislative Chambers," *International Journal of Intercultural Relations* 4 (1980): 367–77.

9. A. Lewis Rhodes, "Effects of Religious Denominations in Occupational Choices," *Sex Roles* 9 (January 1983): 93–108; Charles W. Peek and Sharon Brown, "Sex Prejudice among White Protestants: Like or Unlike Ethnic Prejudice," *Social Forces* 59 (September 1980): 169–85; Brian Powell and Lola Carr Steelman, "Fundamentalism and Sexism," *Social Forces* 60 (June 1982): 676–84.

10. Susan J. Carroll, *Women as Candidates in American Politics* (Bloomington: Indiana University Press, 1985), indicates that on a number of feminist issues, Democratic and Republican women embrace different policy positions. See Clyde Wilcox and Elizabeth Adell Cook, "Evangelical Women and Feminism," *Women and Politics* 9, No. 1 (1989): 27–49; and Clyde Wilcox, "Lingering Support for the Christian Right: Robertsonand Christian Groups in 1988," Paper presented at the 1990 Annual Meeting of the Midwest Political Science Association, Chicago, Illinois, for the negative relationships (and some positive) between conservative Protestants and feminists, liberals, homosexuals, and the abortion issue.

11. Darcy et al., *Women, Elections, and Representation*; Virginia Sapiro, *The Political Integration of Women* (Urbana: University of Illinois Press, 1983); Paula Dubeck, "Women and Access to Political Office," *The Sociological Quarterly* 17 (1976): 42–52; Diamond, *Sex Roles.*

12. This poll was reported in the *Christian Science Monitor* (May 1, 1984), p. 19.

13. Darcy et al., *Women, Elections, and Representation.*

14. Darcy et al., ibid.

15. Rule, "Why Women Don't Run."

16. Carroll, *Women as Candidates,* p. 148.

17. Rule, "Why Women Don't Run."

18. Anderson, "Working Women."

19. I think it is generally recognized that the uniqueness of the South does tend to skew some findings, although they are appropriate in their effects. See Raymond D. Gastil, *Cultural Regions of the United States* (Seattle: University of Washington Press, 1975); Elazar, *American Federalism*.

20. See Susan Welch, "Recruitment of Women to Public Office," *Western Political Quarterly* 31 (September 1978): 372–80. The traditional eligibility pool has generally been in the professions of law and business. However, it has expanded to meet new roles government has begun to perform in the "Great Society" programs of the late 1960s. These new professions are in education, social work, and, to show to what extent barriers have changed within a generation, housewives.

21. Elazar, *American Federalism*; David R. Mayhew, *Placing Parties in American Politics* (Princeton: Princeton University Press, 1986). It is interesting to note that Elazar's individualistic states' cultural values emphasize party competition and that these states are generally large northern industrial states, which Mayhew refers to as traditional party organization states.

22. Peverill Squire, "Career Opportunities and Membership Stability in Legislatures," *Legislative Studies Quarterly* 13 (February 1988): 60–77. Also see Elder Witt, "Are Our Governments Paying What It Takes to Keep the Best and the Brightest?" *Governing* 2 (December 1988): 30–39. Wilma Rule, "Why Women Don't Run," finds some indirect evidence for this assumption, it was not found in work reported by Darcy et al., *Women, Elections, and Representation*.

23. Rule, "Why Women Don't Run"; Darcy et al., *Women, Elections, and Representation*. One should note that Rule's variable is based on the proportion of males who have incomes below, I believe, $8,000. The larger that percentage, the less likely women will do well in state legislatures. Simply using legislative salaries as reported in Darcy et al. does not address the concept of incentives.

24. Mayhew, *Placing Parties*.

25. James Jennings and Monte Rivera, eds., *Puerto Rican Politics in Urban America* (Westport: Greenwood Press, 1984); Maxine Howe, "Latin Politicians Focus on Registration Effort," *New York Times*, Section B, March 30, 1984, p. 1.

26. Thomas D. Boswell and James R. Curtis, *The Cuban-American Experience: Culture, Images, and Perspectives* (Totowa, NJ: Rowman and Allanheld, 1984).

27. Leo Grabler, Joan W. Moore, and Ralph C. Guzman, *The Mexican-American People: The Nation's Second Largest Minority* (New York: Free Press, 1970); Rodolfo O. De la Garza et al., eds., *The Mexican-American Experience: An Interdisciplinary Approach.* (Austin: University of Texas Press, 1985); F. Chris Garcia and Rodolfo O. De la Garza, *The Chicano Experience: Three Perspectives* (North Scituate: Duxbury Press, 1977); "Los Angeles Comes of Age," *The Economist*, April 3, 1982, p. 12.

28. William C. Matney, *America's Black Population 1970 to 1982: A Statistical View* (Washington, D.C.: U.S. Government Printing Office, 1983), p. 3.

29. Peek and Brown, "Sex Prejudices."

30. Bureau of Census Current Population Reports, *Population Profile of the United States, 1982*, Series P-23, No. 130 (Washington, D.C.: U.S. Government Printing Office, 1982).

31. James R. Shortridge, "A New Regionalization of American Religion," *Journal for the Scientific Study of Religion* 16 (June 1977): 143–54. One should note that Bernard Quinn et al., *Churches and Church Membership in the U.S., 1980*

(Atlanta: Glenmary Research Center, 1982), do not differentiate Roman Catholics in this manner.

32. Wayne L. Francis and James Riddlesperger, "U.S. State Legislative Committee Systems: Structure, Procedural Efficiency, and Party Control," *Legislative Studies Quarterly* 7 (1982): 453–71; Alan Rosenthal, *Legislative Life* (New York: Harper & Row, 1981): 163–93 passim.

33. See Darcy et al., *Women, Elections, and Representation*; Richard G. Niemi and Laura Winsky, "Membership Turnover in the U.S. Legislatures," *Legislative Studies Quarterly* 12 (February 1987): 115–24.

34. Quinn et al., *Churches and Church Membership in the U.S.*

3

REPRESENTATION WITHIN POLITICAL PARTIES: A GENDER COMPARISON

Comparisons between genders have been made before, but none sought to perform a longitudinal analysis of minority representation within parties. Explaining genders' representation within parties will prove to be an important element in assessing their influence on policy in future chapters.[1] In addition, due to the small mean percentages of blacks and Hispanics within chambers, comparing gender differences did not yield analytical richness. "Stretching-out" the variations in mean representation with parties makes this possible.

Analytically, the structure of Chapter 3 is similar to that of the preceding chapter. Descriptive statistics of gender differences within groups by party attachment and year are analyzed first. A series of regression analyses follow in order to explain and compare differences in representation. I am assuming that the explanations of representation within parties will not be very different from representation as a percent of full chamber membership.[2]

DESCRIBING MINORITY REPRESENTATION IN PARTIES

Table 3.1 indicates some remarkable stability in group representation within political parties. This is particularly true of Democratic white males (there are a few Asians and American Indians in this group) and Republican white males. In the case of the latter, they actually increased their representation somewhat. Females, other than blacks and Hispanics, slightly increased their representation in their respective parties. Although the shifts in representation are not particularly large, it is interesting to note that Democratic female representation rose during the presidential election; then it fell. Republican female representation, which actually grew more than Democratic females from 1983 to 1987, fell during the presidential election and increased in 1987.

The minorities, blacks and Hispanics, saw their representation decline from 1983 to 1987. Other than the broad assessment of total decline in their respective parties, the small percentages and shifts make patterns difficult to discern. There was one exception, Democratic Hispanic males, whose representation increased from 1983 to 1985, returned to its 1983 level in 1987. These minorities' total representation within the Democratic Party actually fell from nearly 12 percent to 10 percent, this in a party with elements of Reverend Jesse Jackson's "rainbow coalition." One-half of a percent decline also occurs among Hispanics in the Republican Party. It should be noted that changes in chamber size and control of chambers could easily affect these groups because they represent such a small percentage of the Democratic and Republican Parties.

There are several explanations for the erosion of minority representation. First, the off-year 1986 election saw the defeat of Republican

TABLE 3.1
Mean Percent Group Representation within the Democratic and Republican Parties, by Election Year

	Democrats during Years		
Groups	1983	1985	1987
Males*	74.6	74.3	74.5
Females*	14.3	14.9	14.8
Black Males	6.1	5.6	5.5
Black Females	2.1	1.9	2.1
Hispanic Males	2.3	2.9	2.3
Hispanic Females	1.2	.2	.4

	Republicans during Years		
Groups	1983	1985	1987
Males*	81.3	82.6	82.8
Females*	16.4	16.2	16.9
Hispanic Males	1.1	.8	.7
Hispanic Females	.3	.4	.2

*These groups do not include blacks or Hispanics.

minorities as their party's fortunes declined. Democratic blacks and Hispanics also lost seats in 1986 when voter turnout was 37 percent of the voting age population. Perhaps the attrition is due to low turnout among the more poorly educated minorities as other ethnics displaced them. Still, one would not expect other racial and ethnic groups to do well unless minority turnout was very low in mixed racial/ethnic districts.

The importance of these shifts in representation indicates an important fact of U.S. politics. Blacks and Hispanics are likely to do well and hold their own within their largely segregated districts, but they have not done well outside their population centers. In this sense, blacks and Hispanics are not fully incorporated within state political communities. The process of systemic integration through party politics is incomplete — it remains an important, ongoing effort within the large, multicultural and multiethnic environments of the United States.

EXPLAINING MINORITY REPRESENTATION IN PARTIES

Black Democratic Representation

Black representation within the Democratic Party is predicted by some of the same independent variables that predicted their representation within chambers. The variance explained by the multiple regression analysis of black male representation is approximately 40 percent (Table 3.2).

Two variables are particularly important in predicting black representation within the Democratic Party: the percent of the population in metropolitan areas (*beta* .48) and the percent of the population with 16 or more years of education (*beta* −.50). As one might expect, blacks will represent states with metropolitan attributes, particularly in the North. The impact of the large northern metropolitan states and the few which exist in the South (Florida and Texas in particular) are responsible for this *beta* weight. If one were to make this assessment within the South it is highly likely that it would not be a significant predictor. The reasons lie with the large black populations that live outside metropolitan areas. The South, of course, has the largest percent of black representation in their legislative chambers.

The interpretation of the education variable is at best ambiguous. The large metropolitan states may reflect this attribute because a large percentage of their populations may be poorly educated and reduce the proportion of the well educated in a state. I think one may assume, however, that black districts within states will likely reflect this condition.

TABLE 3.2
Multiple Regression Analyses of Black Representation in the Democratic Party, by Gender*

Independent Variables	Gender and Betas	
	Males	Females
Females Employed	.24 d	.28 c
Hispanic Population	.30 c	.28 d
Black Population	.40 a	.17 NS
Democratic Orgns.	.15 NS	.29 c
Cons. Protestants	−.23 c	−.17 NS
Educ. 16 Years +	−.50 a	−.41 a
Metropolitan Population	.48 a	.38 b
Roman Catholic	−.31 b	−.30 c
Traditionalistic	−.39 c	−.32 d
R square	.40	.23

Notes: a = T-test sig. < .001; b = T-test sig. < .01; c = T-test sig. < .05; d = T-test sig. < .10; NS = not significant.

*Analyses include only those independent variables that significantly predict either or both genders' representation in the Democratic Party.

Black male representation is also predicted by black (*beta* .40) and Hispanic (*beta* .30) populations, which generally reside in large metropolitan states. It would appear that the large percentage of black citizens in Elazar's traditionalistic southern culture (*beta* −.39) is not as politicized as its northern, metropolitan counterpart.[3] One should note that participation in voter turnout in these states is often well below the national average.

The percent of females employed is an interesting predictor, albeit of marginal significance (*beta* .24). In Chapter 2, I indicated that this independent variable reflects on the openness of state systems. One may infer that the success of women in the marketplace is similarly linked to black politicization.

If the existence of an open marketplace facilitates black male representation, religious and party variables predicting black representation indicate political barriers to their success. The negative *beta* (−.31) with Roman Catholicism indicates the political conflict that exists within metropolitan areas. Although the *beta* (.15) associated with local

Democratic organizations is not significant, it does indicate that black males are likely to do better where these organizations are weak. The relationship with Roman Catholicism is obvious because most metropolitan organizations, although now in decline, generally were dominated by Roman Catholic ethnics. These relationships indicate the difficult splits in the Democratic Party and, in part, its decline in presidential elections. The party is further fragmented by the relationship between conservative Protestants and black representation (*beta* .23). This is in part related to the conflict over civil rights in the South, but generally we can probably indicate that both religious variables concern social intolerance as well as the struggle for political power.[4]

A regression analysis (Table 3.2) of black female representation explains only 23 percent of the variance, far less than that predicting male success. This is due to the small percentage of black females in the Democratic Party and implies that we should treat these findings with greater caution.

Many of the independent variables that predicted black male representation also predict female representation. This is to be expected because they reside in similar demographic areas, but there are some differences. Black females are likely to represent states with metropolitan attributes (*beta* .38) in which a smaller percentage of the population will have 16 or more years of education (*beta* .41). The metropolitan nature of black female success is found in the positive, but marginal, relationship found with Hispanics (*beta* .28, sig. < .10). There is an insignificant, but positive, relationship found with the number of blacks (*beta* .17). Although these independent variables are weaker than those for males, it is likely due to the small percentages of females found in state legislatures. As their political success increases, I think these variables will become more strongly related to their representation within the Democratic Party.

Regional, religious, and party variables also represent significant barriers to black female success. Because they represent states with metropolitan attributes, their success is predicated on the existence of weak, local Democratic organizations (*beta* .29). This variable does not significantly predict male success (although there is a positive relationship), and for this reason I would suggest that, like other females, black female training probably occurred in voluntary and community service work. An additional probable factor explaining the development of their leadership skills is that more black women are active in their local churches. Steven Peterson has indicated that strong church participation also increases politicization, and I think this could be extended to other interests.[5] Each of these experiences is likely to develop political skills and translate into the development of candidate-centered organizations. These organizations are more successful if local Democratic organizations are weak.

A relationship between weak Democratic party organizations and representation is clarified by the inverse relationship found with the proportion of Roman Catholics in states (*beta* −.30). This relationship is equal to that associated with males and indicates the political conflict between Roman Catholic ethnics, their party organizations, and emerging black political strength in metropolitan areas. Not only does this represent intraparty conflict, but one must also recognize the social intolerance based on racism in U.S. society.

A Roman Catholic population is not the only barrier to black female success; a southern traditionalistic political subculture also represents an important barrier (*beta* .32). This is due in part to low political participation found in this subculture and to conservative Protestantism. There is an inverse relationship (*beta* −.17 NS) with black female success, but it is not significant. Again, the small proportion of black women in state legislatures has influenced the regression analysis. I think one may infer there is social intolerance among members of the Christian Right.[6]

Although there are some gender differences, we can summarize that the major factors predicting their success are quite similar. State attributes associated with metropolitan areas are obvious predictors as is the sensitivity of female political success to the female employed in state economies. This variable does marginally predict male representation, but it is more important to females. In a real sense, it reflects a degree of openness in the states and may have a temporary predictive effect. Let us assume that it represents a transition period in the further development of U.S. society and its economy. As all states modernize, variations in the numbers of women employed will decrease. I think it likely that this variable will have less capacity to differentiate women's and minorities' political success.

The party, religious, and regional variables are also important barriers to black representation. Strong Democratic organizations do not recruit blacks for legislative office, but the displacement of Roman Catholic ethnics and their party organizations predicts black success. As such, these factors reflect the fragmentation of the Democratic Party, and one may infer this is one reason it is unlikely to win a presidential election very soon.

Hispanic Democratic Representation

Hispanic representation in the Democratic Party reveals a pattern found in the regression analyses of black representation. The variance explained for males and females is 51 percent and 20 percent, respectively, indicating that the small percentage of women engenders some caution while interpreting the results (see Table 3.3). Fortunately, the independent variables predicting male and female representation are similar, thus strengthening the interpretation of these findings.

The paucity of strong predictors among males is also a function of very small percentages represented in the Democratic Party. Among the seven independent variables that predict Hispanic representation, a large Hispanic population (*beta* .79) is the major predictor of male representation. Were it not for this very strong predictor, the variance explained would probably be nominal. With the exception of this variable, only two other variables significantly predict male political success, size of legislative districts and the percent of the population with 16 or more years of education. Three other variables marginally predict male success, and these reflect the conflicts within metropolitan areas: metropolitan attributes and Roman Catholicism, which I relate to European ethnics.

TABLE 3.3
Multiple Regression Analyses of Hispanic Representation in the Democratic Party, by Gender*

Independent Variables	Gender and Betas	
	Males	Females
Hispanic Population	.79 a	.24 d
Females Employed	.14 NS	.25 d
District Size	−.34 a	−.15 NS
Democratic Orgns.	.22 d	.25 d
Educ. 16 Years +	−.23 c	−.40 b
Metropolitan Population	.20 d	.38 b
Roman Catholic	−.21 d	−.27 d
R square	.51	.20

Notes: a = T-test sig. < .001; b = T-test sig. < .01; c = T-test sig. < .05; d = T-test sig. < .10; NS = not significant.

*Analyses include only those independent variables that significantly predict either or both genders' representation in the Democratic Party.

Hispanic males are likely to represent states that, in addition to a large Hispanic population, have smaller legislative districts (*beta* −.34). For females, no significant relationship exists between the size of districts and their representation, although an inverse relationship does exist. This does not mean that Hispanic males are less competitive than other groups in legislative politics. Rather, this research artifact is due to the effect of New Mexico, which skews the regression analysis. Males do very well in New Mexico, which has a very large Hispanic population, and it should be noted that in this traditionalistic state, women do not do as well politically. Therefore, female representation in the Democratic Party is only marginally predicted by a Hispanic population (*beta* .24, sig. < .10).

New Mexico, however, is not a metropolitan state. The remaining variables predicting male and female success symbolize the conflict of political displacement in metropolitan states. Metropolitan attributes only marginally predict male success but do significantly predict female success (*betas*: males, .20, sig. < .10; females, .38). The difference is due to the skewed effect of New Mexico, but the significant relationship of a less well-educated population (*betas*: males, −.23; females, −.40) for both genders indicates that metropolitan representation is likely to become more important. One must remember that 65 percent of all Hispanics reside in a small number of large metropolitan states. Since they do, conflict with European Roman Catholic ethnics is implied by the relationships between local Democratic organizations (*betas*: males, .22, sig. < .10; females, .25, sig. < .10) and Roman Catholicism. Hispanics do relatively well when local Democratic organizations are weak and when there are fewer European Roman Catholic ethnics. Hispanics are Roman Catholics and are likely to support members of their communities. It is highly likely that the Glenmary publication, which relies on the Roman Catholic church's estimates of communicant members, may be flawed. It is likely that these estimates may not include many new Hispanic immigrants. As super Catholics with cultural values associated with the lands of their birth, they may feel out of place in a U.S. Catholic church.[7] If this is true, European ethnics, which have long dominated metropolitan areas, are probably fighting a rearguard action to prevent being displaced by Democratic Hispanics and blacks.

As in earlier findings, Hispanic females are likely to be represented in states where female employment is higher (*beta* .25, sig. < .10). This is a marginal relationship, due I think to the small percentage of females, and it should be noted that it does not significantly predict male representation, although a positive relationship is evident. For fear of repeating myself one must assume the important effects employment has for women. Involvement in the work force increases political interest and participation.

Summarizing the relative success of Hispanics, it would seem females are not likely to be represented in states with large Hispanic populations. Males are represented in these populations, but they seem less likely to be represented in states with metropolitan attributes. These findings are due in part to the skewed effect of traditionalistic New Mexico's large Hispanic population and its extensive representation in the legislature. When one has small percentages of minorities, the likelihood of the findings being skewed is greater. For this reason, correlational analyses using state characteristics to explain representation always include a good deal of interpretive ambiguity. Which findings can one take literally? The relationships between metropolitan, party, and religious variables indicate the conflict with displaced populations that figures so importantly in metropolitan areas. A real difference is found where females are employed. Not only does this represent openness; it also reflects a complex process of politicization leading to successful participation in state legislatures.

Hispanic Republican Representation

The regression analyses of Hispanic success in the Republican Party include five independent variables that significantly predict either or both genders' representation in the Republican Party. However, the small percentages of both genders' representation means that only 21 percent and 18 percent of the variance was explained for males and females, respectively. If it were not for the similarity in predictor variables, I would be extremely cautious in accepting these findings. Still, the reader should remain somewhat cautious.

Table 3.4 reveals four significant independent variables predicting male and female success in the Republican Party. A reason for some caution in this analysis rests with the insignificant effect of the Hispanic population (*beta* .20, NS) to predict male success, but the population does significantly (*beta* .30) predict female political success. It would appear that during this election period, males were somewhat successful in areas where there were smaller Hispanic populations. This is not true of females where a significant relationship exists.

Although males have done somewhat better beyond large Hispanic population centers, the evidence indicates that they do better in large metropolitan states (*beta* .40) and where the population is likely to be less well educated in terms of a university education (*beta* −.35). Females also

TABLE 3.4
Multiple Regression Analyses of Hispanic Representation in
the Republican Party, by Gender*

	Gender and Betas	
Independent Variables	Males	Females
Hispanic Population	.79 a	.24 d
Cons. Protestants	−.33 b	−.20 NS
Educ. 16 Years +	−.35 c	−.44 a
Metropolitan Population	.42 c	.34 c
Roman Catholic	−.30 c	−.27 d
R square	.21	.20

Notes: a = T-test sig. < .001; b = T-test sig. < .01; c = T-test sig. < .05; d = T-test sig. < .10; NS = not significant.

*Analyses include only those independent variables that significantly predict either or both genders' representation in the Republican Party.

do well in metropolitan states (*beta* .34) and in states with a smaller percentage of the population with a university education (*beta* −.44). The percent of the population with 16 or more years of education is a state attribute that would seem to be an unlikely predictor of Hispanic success. However, Cuban Hispanics, who initially immigrated to the United States in the early 1960s, represent a better educated and skilled group than, for example, Puerto Ricans and late arriving Mexican-Americans. As a group they are better educated, politically active as conservatives, and anti-Communists.

Both genders also do poorly if the Roman Catholic population is large (*betas*: males, −.30; females, −.26, sig. < .10). Again, I am certain that Hispanic Republicans are being elected by Roman Catholic constituencies, but I do not believe that the true number of Hispanic Catholics may be included in my data sources. One may interpret this relationship to mean that there is political conflict between these new immigrants and existing European or other Hispanic ethnics who are probably being displaced politically in metropolitan areas. In addition, conservative Protestants also seem to be a barrier to male Hispanics (*beta* −.33) but much less a barrier for females (*beta* .20, NS). These relationships are similar to those associated with blacks in the Democratic Party, but there is a larger partisan element to be found. Traditionally, conservative white Protestants in the South vote Democratic in state legislative elections.

However, I would not entirely rule out the possibility of social intolerance. It is simply more difficult to interpret what really are statistically weak regression analyses. The weakness of these analyses is found in the variables that do not significantly predict their success in the Republican Party: the females employed in state economies and local Democratic organizations.

These variables have been significant in the analyses in Chapter 2, but they fail to be reflected here. This should raise a cautionary flag concerning the findings associated with the very small numbers of Hispanic Republicans in U.S. state legislatures.

EXPLAINING OTHER LEGISLATOR REPRESENTATION IN PARTIES

For purposes of symmetry, gender comparisons between other legislators, most of them white, would seem appropriate. Using a similar methodological approach, the following regression analyses assess male and female representation within the Republican and Democratic Parties.

Republican Representation

Ten independent variables predict one or both genders' representation within the Republican Party. The regression analyses explain 49 percent of the variance associated with male representation and 40 percent for females. The variance explained, although somewhat different, is very close to the variance explained by Republican female representation within chambers (Chapter 2).

There are quite a number of differences that explain male and female representation within the Republican Party. Three major differences will catch the reader's attention (see Table 3.5). First, metropolitan areas predict female success but not male success, which is likely to occur in all Republican environments (see Table 3.1). Second, there are very real differences in the party variables predictive capacities, and, of course, there is the effect of female employment on their political success in state legislatures.

Table 3.5 indicates that female employment is one of the most important variables predicting female success (*beta* .36). The percent of females employed in the states has often been a significant predictor of minority representation, whether male or female, regardless of party attachments. The only exceptions have been Hispanic Republicans, but there the regression analyses are quite weak. I have interpreted this factor to be

TABLE 3.5
Multiple Regression Analyses of All Other Legislators'
Representation in the Republican Party, by Gender*

Independent Variables	Gender and Betas	
	Males	Females
Females Employed	−.04 NS	.36 b
Chamber Reduced	−.20 b	.18 c
Committee Chairs	−.20 c	−.02 NS
District Size	.18 d	−.18 NS
Democratic Orgns.	.45 a	−.08 NS
Cons. Protestants	.45 a	−.38 a
Educ. 16 Years +	−.14 NS	−.26 c
Trad. Party Orgns.	.32 a	−.20 d
Metropolitan Population	−.01 NS	.26 c
Republican Orgns.	−.25 c	.11 NS
R square	.49	.40

Notes: a = T-test sig. < .001; b = T-test sig. < .01; c = T-test sig. < .05; d = T-test sig. < .10; NS = not significant.

*Analyses only include those independent variables that predict either or both genders' representation in the Republican Party. Please note that this table represents males and females other than Hispanics.

representative of systemic openness, and this analysis reinforces that assumption. Female employment can be interpreted to increase female politicization, for example, political interest and efficacy, and is therefore a major predictor of Republican female political success. What makes this an important element of systemic openness is that it has no significant impact on a sizable white group of Republican males (*beta* .04 NS).

Generally, females are more likely to be successful in metropolitan states (*beta* .26) that are less likely to have a large percentage of the population with a college education (*beta* −.26). I think it is apparent that Republican females do not represent central cities. Rather they are likely to represent well-educated suburban areas of metropolitan states. This introduces one element of interpretive ambiguity associated with using statewide variables to predict political success: large metropolitan states may have a lower proportion of well-educated citizens, but this would be untrue of suburban areas. Neither of these independent variables predicts male success, but males are likely to represent states with large legislative districts (*beta* .18, sig. < .10). This suggests that they probably do well in all states regardless of their metropolitan virtues. Success in states with large districts seems to suggest that males may be more competitive than females. Although this variable did not significantly predict female success, it was nearly marginally significant, and the *beta* weight was a positive .18. I would urge caution in leaping to the conclusion that females in the Republican Party may not be very competitive. The truth is that in Illinois where the chamber size was reduced, males lost representation (*beta* −.20) while females gained (*beta* .18) in what was a very competitive political environment.

Any assessment of Republican political success would imply that strong local Republican organizations coupled with weak Democratic organizations would be logical. Indeed, Republican male representation is predicted by strong local Republican organizations (*beta* −.25) and weak Democratic organizations (*beta* .45). In fact, a weak local Democratic party is one of the major predictors of male success. So far, this is appropriate, until one assesses Republican female success. First, a local Democratic organization has no significant effect on the likely success of a female. Nor does a local Republican party organization, and what is quite interesting is that there is some intimation that a weak organization may be preferable to female representation (*beta* .11, NS). Clearly, the pattern of female representation has little to do with local Republican support. This could be due to weak, rather independent suburban organizations, but it is highly likely that candidate-centered organizations remain most important to a female's success. Indeed, one may posit that her political experience derives from local volunteer organizations and not the Republican Party. The same cannot be said for males who do well when the opposition party is weak and the Republican Party is efficacious. In addition, a Republican male is likely to do well in traditional party organization states (*beta* .32), but not a female (*beta* .20, sig. < .10).

Each of these factors indicates the impact of parties. Research in the past has indicated that where the Democratic Party is dominant, a female will face a significant barrier to her success.[8] Unfortunately, Rule's research (and much other research) does not differentiate party attachments of female groups and leaves one with the assumption that only a Democratic organization is likely to oppose female political success. Neither party, as you will see, must be doing much for their female aspirants.

The other major predictor of Republican male success is the percentage of conservative Protestants in a state. If the percentage is high, white Republican males do very well (*beta* .45), but white females do not (*beta* –.38). In fact, conservative Protestants represent the most important predictor of female success. Females are doing better in northern suburban communities, but this raises an interesting question. In the 1970s, they seemed to do much better in the rather homogeneous, moralistic subcultural states. Their representation in larger metropolitan states may reflect the conservative era, whose values are antithetical to female political interests and representation.

Finally, I had assumed that the larger the number of committee chairs, the greater the inducement to enter the legislature. This assumed that the likelihood of affecting legislation in committees would be greater. For males, this was not the case. A negative *beta* (–.20) indicates that males are likely to be represented in chambers with fewer chairs as a percent of the total chamber membership. (No significant relationship exists for females.) This is quite intriguing because they also represent states with larger legislative districts. It is difficult to place a clear interpretation on this, other than to note the attribute. The question must be whether this variable predicts turnover and in what sense it would do so. Then, one might question the effect it would have on political power within legislative chambers.

Democratic Representation

Table 3.6 indicates that ten independent variables predict either or both genders' representation within the Democratic Party. The variance explained for Democratic males and females is .50 and .49, respectively.

Several interesting points must be made about the predictors of Democratic representation. First, states with metropolitan attributes do not predict either genders' representation. This is unusual. Traditionally, metropolitan areas and states, especially in the Northeast, have manifested a Democratic bias. Second, as we compare genders within the Democratic Party, it is important to recognize that Democratic females face extreme barriers from traditional supporters. This is probably associated with the conservatism of this era. Various social issues, for example, abortion, are anathema to traditional values espoused by conservative groups. Other relevant factors have been reported in Chapter 2 and are discussed below.

Openness in the United States seems to be related to the number of females employed. Whether minority and regardless of party attachment, this factor predicts political participation. However, the percent females employed does not predict either Democratic or Republican male success. That is to be expected, but like other minorities, this independent variable

TABLE 3.6
Multiple Regression Analyses of All Other Legislators' Representation in the Democratic Party, by Gender*

Independent Variables	Gender and Betas	
	Males	Females
Females Employed	−.02 NS	.24 c
Hispanic Population	−.69 a	.02 NS
Chamber Shifts Repub.	.12 d	−.03 NS
Multimember Dist.	−.12 NS	.16 d
Chamber to Dems.	.13 d	−.07 NS
Democratic Orgns.	−.02 NS	.19 d
Black Population	−.23 c	_.11 NS
Cons. Protestants	.29 b	−.37 a
Roman Catholic	.17 NS	−.33 b
Traditionalistic	.27 d	−.35 c
R square	.50	.49

Notes: a = T-test sig. < .001; b = T-test sig. < .01; c = T-test sig. < .05; d = T-test sig. < .10; NS = not significant.

*Analyses include only those independent variables that predict either or both genders' representation in the Democratic Party. Please note that this table represents males and females other than blacks and Hispanics.

predicts female success (*beta* .24) indicating how crucial this variable is to the development of political interest and participation. I believe that is not merely a phenomenon affecting only women. When males find that females are competent in the marketplace, barriers to their political ambitions may be lowered. However, one may infer that the cultivation of their political skills has occurred in voluntary work and political organizations created to deal with local and state issues. A reason for this is quite simple: development of interest and support for political office does not come for the Democratic Party. The analysis below indicates females do better when local Democratic organizations are weak (*beta* .19, sig. < .10). This, I think, is due to the barrier attached to traditional supporters of Democratic candidates, North and South.

Traditional supporters of Democrats have always been Roman Catholic ethnics and southern Protestants. The latter generally vote Republican in presidential elections, but they continue to support Democrats in state legislative elections. However, these groups represent serious barriers to Democratic females' representation within their party.

Female success is predicted if there are smaller conservative Protestant (*beta* −.37) and Roman Catholic (*beta* −.33) populations. The conservative Protestant population represents a positive relationship (*beta* .29) with males, as does the Roman Catholic population although the *beta* is insignificant. I think the position of these groups has much to do with the conservative era that has dominated the political agenda during the Reagan years, in particular the issue of abortion. Many Roman Catholics and conservative Protestants oppose abortion on religious grounds. It is probably not too extreme to assert that this issue, among others, represents a conflict between good and evil, God and the anti-Christ.

Other factors come into play for conservative Protestants, and perhaps for many Roman Catholics, as well. For example, conservative Protestants have a visceral dislike for feminists and liberals in addition to liberal female politicians' support for abortion. Although not all Democratic females may take what conservatives refer to as extreme positions, stereotypically Democrats are viewed as liberals. There is evidence for making this assumption. Generally, Democratic females are more likely to support a whole range of what Susan Carroll refers to as feminist issues.[9] Unfortunately, Democratic women must seek traditional votes from Roman Catholics and conservative Protestants in the South. While both groups still vote Democratic in state legislative elections, they seem to be important gatekeepers that have stymied female political success. The evidence of lack of support is also found in the inverse relationship between Elazar's traditionalistic subculture and female representation (*beta* −.35). This is a subculture identified with the South and border states where Democratic female representation has declined during the 1980s. Males, as the above religious variables indicate, have no such problems in a traditionalistic subculture (*beta* .27). They do quite well in the South's state legislatures. With these factors in mind, it is no wonder that Democratic female representation was stagnant during the 1980s; in fact, it declined slightly.

One remaining variable predicts Democratic female success, multimember districts. R. Darcy et al. indicate that a multimember district plan should benefit women; however, this type of district representation has thus far been found to be a major predictor of black representation in the South.[10] Other than that instance, this represents one case in which a multimember district plan, at least marginally, predicted female success (*beta* .16, sig. < .10). As expected, this plan of representation does not significantly predict male success. Indeed, the insignificant *beta* represents an inverse relationship (−.12, NS). I think the use of a different methodological strategy, and emphasizing the likely effects of religious and political variables, may have thrust this variable into the background. In any case it does not represent a major factor predicting female success generally (see Chapter 2).

Male success is largely predicted if the Hispanic (*beta* −.69) and black (*beta* −.23) populations are quite small. Female success is not significantly affected by these variables either. This is quite surprising because Democratic support is perceived to be greater in metropolitan areas. The Hispanic population is found in several major metropolitan states controlled by the Democratic Party to some extent, at least the General Assembly or House of Representatives. Each of these inverse relationships with the minority population represents the reason Democratic male success is not found to be statistically significant in metropolitan states.

Competition for political power is likely to occur when a change in chamber control is likely to occur. If a chamber becomes Democratic, male Democrats ought to do well, and they do (*beta* .13, sig. < .10). One might expect the same to be true for female success, but a very weak, insignificant inverse relationship exists. In addition, a change of chamber control to the Republican Party also has a marginal, but significant impact on male representation (*beta* .12, sig. < .10). An extremely weak, insignificant relationship exists for women. Does this suggest that to some extent in periods of political change males do better than females? Table 2.4 in Chapter 2 indicates a similar insignificant and inverse relationship for Democratic females in the North. It is difficult to ascribe a lack of competitiveness, suggested by a peer, when so many other factors come into play, for example, obtaining party support and funds to run a viable campaign during political uncertainty.

Some relationships are clear; the intolerance of conservative voting groups within the Democratic Party: conservative Protestants and Roman Catholics. These relationships indicate the significant barriers that Democratic women must overcome within their own party. Males, of course, do not face these barriers. Much of the problem lies with the conservative era that has dominated the political agenda. Conservative Protestants have a strong dislike for liberals and feminists; hence, the negative *beta* is easily interpreted. Democratic women are more liberal on women's issues, and stereotypically they are perceived as feminists. The interpretations one may offer are varied, but social intolerance, religious values, and general conflict over an array of substantive and symbolic issues are highly likely. These relationships may change in the future if the political agenda were to be directed toward a liberal agenda, for example, issues associated with education and homeless families and citizens. Such an agenda would at least favor women's success with Roman Catholics.[11]

Males who do well among conservative Protestants (but not as well as Republican males), the traditionalistic subculture, and somewhat better with Roman Catholics are not similarly affected. Of course, politics is traditionally viewed as a male function, but also they probably can escape the liberalism attached to female Democrats.

Finally, the impact of females employed in the states is a critically important predictor of Democratic female success. The interpretation that this leads to political interest, efficacy, and participation is entirely appropriate. In a larger context, it is also a significant predictor for most minorities, male or female, regardless of party attachments. The variable seems to indicate systemic openness necessary to minority and other female success.

NOTES

1. I think that Susan J. Carroll, *Women as Candidates in American Politics* (Bloomington: Indiana University Press, 1985), makes the important policy distinctions between women of different parties that provide the reasons for my analyses. Her work on issues and the literature on political parties clarifies the need to differentiate between parties. Following this line of thought, it would seem appropriate to explain representation within parties as well, particularly the differences within minority groups associated with gender.

2. Comparisons within regions is still not possible, particularly in the South. This is due in large part to the very small percentages of minority females, notably among Hispanics.

3. Daniel J. Elazar, *American Federalism: A View from the States* (New York: Thomas Y. Crowell, 1972).

4. Clyde Wilcox, "Lingering Support for the Christian Right: Robertson and the Christian Right Groups in 1988." Paper presented at the 1990 Annual Meeting of the Midwest Political Science Association, Chicago, Illinois. In this paper Wilcox indicates the basic dislike conservative Protestants have for liberals, often black politicians, and, of course, feminists. Charles W. Peek and Sharon Brown, "Sex Prejudice among White Protestants: Like or Unlike Ethnic Prejudice," *Social Forces* 59 (September 1980): 169–85, have dealt with similar themes. Also see Brian Powell and Lola Carr, "Fundamentalism and Sexism," *Social Forces* 60 (June 1982): 676–84.

5. Steven A. Peterson, "Church Participation and Political Participation: The Spillover Effect." Paper delivered at the 1990 Annual Meeting of the Midwest Political Science Association, Chicago, Illinois. He does not differentiate genders, and I am assuming two things: first, the importance of black churches to the black communities; and second, females may be more devout than males and, therefore, more active within their respective churches.

6. See Elazar, *American Federalism*; Wilcox, "Lingering Support"; Peek and Brown, "Sex Prejudice"; Powell and Carr, "Fundamentalism and Sexism."

7. James R. Shortridge, "A New Regionalization of American Religion," *Journal for the Scientific Study of Religion* 16 (June 1977): 143–54, differentiates the Hispanic and French populations as "super Catholics." Bernard Quinn et al., *Churches and Church Membership in the U.S.* (Atlanta: Glenmary Research Center, 1982), do not differentiate between Hispanic Catholics and others.

8. See Wilma Rule, "Why Women Don't Run," *Western Political Quarterly* 34 (March 1984): 60–77; R. Darcy, Susan Welch, and Janet Clark, *Women, Elections, and Representation* (New York: Longman, 1987).

9. Carroll, *Women as Candidates*; Wilcox, "Lingering Support."

10. Darcy et al., *Women, Elections, and Representation*, pp. 125–26.

11. See John R. Petrocik, "Issues and Agendas: Electoral Coalitions in the 1988 Election." Paper delivered at the 1989 Annual Meeting of the American Political Science Association, Atlanta, Georgia. His paper indicates the effects of successful Republican control of the issue agenda (at least symbolically), which depreciated the potential appeal of social welfare issues to many groups in the 1988 presidential campaign.

4

TURNOVER IN LOWER STATE LEGISLATIVE CHAMBERS

Incorporation is concerned with entry and access to political authority found in institutions. Just as important as representation, turnover can affect the collective influence of a minority group. The assumption is quite simple: large turnover indicates that fewer members will develop the legislative and policy expertise to serve their constituents and states. Of course, not everyone will find the legislature conducive to their interests, but the evidence suggests turnover has been declining since the 1930s. I also assume that most turnover in U.S. state legislatures is not due to electoral defeat; few incumbents are defeated for reelection. Other reasons dictate leaving the legislature: fed up with a process associated with incremental policy making, death or illness, social mobility in politics, strain on family ties, or a recognition in a competitive district that certain defeat can be circumvented by leaving office.[1]

In order to appraise the variation among these minority groups, I focus on descriptive statistics to portray turnover within chambers during each election year. A comparison is made of party and minority group turnover and of the percentage of each group that changes with each election. I also portray the differences in northern and southern states.

Finally, I explain turnover within chambers, both political parties, and the turnover of each minority group using similar independent variables with multiple regression analysis. By comparing the results of each regression analysis during this period, one should be able to ascertain the various factors that affect turnover for each group.

TURNOVER IN ELECTION YEARS

Evidence has been cited that turnover has declined since the 1930s in legislative chambers. Table 4.1 indicates that turnover is more complex than a single downward curve. Turnover was unusually high in 1983 (32.0 percent) during the 1981 to 1983 recession and reapportionment years. However, there is really no difference in the turnover of each party. Democratic turnover was at 15.9 percent and Republican turnover stood at 16.0 percent. In 1983, one would have expected the Republicans to lose more seats because their party held the White House and would be blamed for economic conditions. In addition, President Ronald Reagan's presidential popularity seriously declined during this period, and one would expect Republican fortunes to flow with this tide of unpopularity.[2]

The unique aspect of this table is that turnover for the Republicans significantly declines to 8.2 percent with the success of their party in the 1984 presidential election. This does not mean that the Democrats do worse in comparison to the 1982 election. Their turnover also declines slightly in 1984 to 14.6 percent, but this is certainly greater than Republican turnover in the same year. One can emphasize that in the 1980s the losing party in the Presidential election did not really do worse, they only suffered by comparison with the winning presidential party.

In the 1986 off-year election, turnover within the two parties is once again quite similar with Republican turnover only slightly worse (0.8 percent difference) in spite of President Reagan's problems in the Iran-Contra scandal and the Republican loss of the U.S. Senate.

Turnover may have a more serious effect in states where parties are quite competitive. In these states turnover may cause changes in party control. The size of the turnover, although similar for both parties, is likely to be quite serious for Republicans in 1982 and, of course, the

TABLE 4.1
Turnover as a Percent of Chambers, by
Party and Election Year

| Election Years | Turnover | | |
	Total	Democrats	Republicans
1982	32.0	15.9	16.0
1984	22.7	14.6	8.2
1986	21.9	10.6	11.4

Iran-Contra scandal of 1986. In Table 4.2, it is apparent that changes to Democratic control occurred during the 1982 election. Nearly 56 percent of the changes to Democratic control occurred during this election, while changes to Republican control (about 57 percent) occurred during the 1984 presidential election. Given the small number of changes (nine for Democrats and seven for Republicans), one cannot really stipulate that the Democrats did better in 1986 when the Reagan administration was embroiled in the Iran-Contra scandal. The administration lost control of the U.S. Senate, but only three Republican legislative chambers became Democratic. Two Democratic chambers turned Republican. One may suggest that economic downturns in this study were more harmful to the administration's party in grassroots state legislative elections, but the scandal did not significantly affect voters' grassroots choices in 1986.

The impact of each election year on our minority groups, in addition to other Democratic and Republican males, is found in Tables 4.3 and 4.4. These tables include not only group turnover as a percent of chamber membership but also the percentage of representation that changes for each group. This allows some comparison, particularly differences between other Democratic and Republican males and each of our minority groups.

Generally, total Democratic turnover noted in Table 4.1 declines over the period of this study. Table 4.3 indicates stable turnover among these minority groups, although one might suggest that Democratic female (other than blacks and Hispanics) turnover declined by over 25 percent from 2.1 percent to 1.5 percent. This decline is matched by that of other Democratic males' turnover from 12.6 percent to 7.9 percent or approximately 37 percent. Turnover among blacks and Hispanics has been stable.

During this period, the turnover of these groups represents a significant percentage of their representation. Generally black turnover as

TABLE 4.2
Changes in Party Control by Year

	Years of Change					
	1982		1984		1986	
Party Success Changed:	NR	%	NR	%	NR	%
To Democrats	(5)	55.6	(1)	11.1	(3)	33.3
To Republicans	(1)	14.3	(4)	57.1	(2)	28.6

TABLE 4.3
Democratic Turnover as a Percent of Chamber Membership Compared to Representation in Chambers, by Group and Year

Year and Group	Representation	Turnover	Turnover as a Percent of Representation
1983			
Other Males*	46.9	12.6	26.8
Other Females*	7.4	2.1	28.3
Blacks	4.1	.8	19.5
Hispanics	1.6	.4	25.0
1984			
Other Males*	43.0	11.5	26.7
Other Females*	7.5	2.2	29.3
Blacks	4.4	.7	15.9
Hispanics	1.6	.3	18.7
1986			
Other Males*	42.8	7.9	18.5
Other Females*	7.8	1.5	19.2
Blacks	4.3	.7	18.6
Hispanics	1.7	.4	23.5

*Other than blacks and Hispanics.

a percentage of representation is lower than that percentage for other groups. Still, it falls between 15.9 percent and 19.5 percent during the three election periods. It is interesting to note that the largest turnover among blacks as a percentage of representation occurs in 1982, a good year for Democrats if one is assessing changes in party control. Turnover is lowest during the 1984 presidential (15.9 percent) election when Republicans as a group did so well politically. The pattern is similar for Hispanics, although a larger percentage of their group leaves office than do blacks. Other male and female turnover as a percentage of their representation is very similar, although female turnover is slightly higher. But the sharpest decline as a percent of representation occurs in 1986, not 1984. The difference may rest on when significant numbers of black and Hispanic voters are likely to turnout. Perhaps this occurs during the more dramatic presidential elections when turnout is significantly greater than it is among the voters supporting other Democratic males and females.

TABLE 4.4
Republican Turnover as a Percent of Chamber Membership
Compared to Representation in Chambers,
by Group and Year

Year and Group	Representation	Turnover	Turnover as a Percent of Representation
1982			
Other Males*	35.1	13.8	39.0
Other Females*	7.0	2.2	31.4
Hispanics	.2	.15	75.0
1984			
Other Males*	38.3	6.8	17.7
Other Females*	7.6	1.4	18.4
Hispanics	.4	.1	25.0
1986			
Other Males*	36.4	9.5	26.1
Other Females*	7.2	1.8	25.0
Hispanics	.3	.1	33.3

*Other than Hispanics.

Turnover among other Republican males and females follows the pattern of Republican turnover found in Table 4.1. This is to be expected because Republican constituent support is less varied than that found within the Democratic Party. Male turnover, 13.8 percent in the 1982 election, falls to 6.8 percent in 1984, better than a 50 percent decline. It increases to 9.5 percent in 1986. Female turnover is 2.2 percent in 1982, falls to 1.4 percent in 1984 (decline of about 36 percent), and increases to 1.8 percent in 1986. Republican Hispanics' turnover remained stable at approximately one-tenth of a percent, although it did decrease from 0.15 percent to 0.1 percent.

Republican females generally have less turnover as a percentage of their representation during the period, although other Republican males' turnover as a percentage of representation was slightly less. In this respect, Republican females seem to have more success than their Democratic sisters across the aisle. However, as we will learn, most legislatures during this period are controlled by the Democratic Party. Hence, Democratic females are actually in a greater position to wield more power than Republican females. Republican males find their turnover as a percent of representation to be 39 percent in 1982, evidence that economic downturns significantly affect the party in power. In fact all three Republican groups suffer extensive turnover as a percentage of representation in the 1982 election. Hispanic turnover as a percentage of representation is greater, although the small percentages make it difficult to assert this is likely to be a pattern in the future.

Generally, in terms of the absolute size of turnover, most turnover occurs among other Democratic and Republican males. In the Democratic Party, other males' turnover is five to six times as great as female turnover. The same is true within the Republican Party. This represents some possibility for female advancement within lower state legislative chambers. Still, women's advancement has not really advanced as rapidly as might be expected if incumbency among white males is the only factor blocking their political advancement. Other factors probably come into play, and these are most likely associated with traditional cultural values during a relatively conservative era. This conservatism, and the social elements supporting it, is a major factor for women's stagnated representation and cannot be resolved by simply increasing turnover among males.

The presidential election's effects in 1984 largely, and positively, affected the Republican Party. Its turnover sharply fell in 1984 and rose to approximate the turnover of the Democratic Party in 1986. Democratic turnover simply continued to decline during each successive year, although the largest decline in turnover occurred in 1986. Table 4.5 indicates some interesting regional differences and some differences between largely white representatives and minorities.

Among Democratic males and females in the North, turnover is very stable in the 1982 and 1984 elections. The decline in turnover as a percent of chambers occurs among blacks and Hispanics; however, for the latter groups, turnover increases in 1986 to the level set in 1982. One must recognize that we are dealing with minute percentages, and, if I am to make these assessments, it should be noted that black turnover was smaller by 0.3 percent in 1986 than it was in 1982. Nevertheless, turnover increased for northern minorities while it declined for other Democratic males and females.

The variation among Democrats in the South is somewhat different. First, other Democratic male turnover declines from 17.6 percent in 1982 to 13.7 percent in 1984 and finally to 10.8 percent in 1986. This clear decline is not shared by other Democratic groups. They are more sensitive to Republican success because their turnover increases in 1984

TABLE 4.5
Turnover within the Democratic and Republican Parties in the North and South, by Election Year
(in percent)

	Democratic Groups			
Region and Year	Males	Females	Hispanics	Blacks
North				
1982	11.1	2.2	0.5	0.8
1984	10.9	2.3	0.3	0.3
1986	7.1	1.6	0.5	0.5
South				
1982	17.6	1.8	0.1	1.1
1984	13.7	2.1	0.5	1.9
1986	10.8	1.1	0.1	1.5

	Republican Groups		
	Males	Females	Hispanics
North			
1982	15.8	2.7	0.2
1984	7.8	1.7	0.03
1986	10.9	2.0	0.1
South			
1982	7.1	0.5	0.1
1984	3.3	0.3	0.2
1986	4.3	0.8	0.1

and declines in 1986. Again, this cautionary note, the variations in turnover are minute, but a pattern emerges that places other Democratic females (white) with other Democratic minorities in the South. And, I must add, that the variation in turnover among these southern minorities is dissimilar. Turnover decreases among northern blacks and Hispanics in 1984, but it increases among Democratic females, blacks, and Hispanics in the South.

Does this mean that increased voter turnout in the South has more serious consequences for incumbents? In the North, Hispanic and black incumbents seem to solidify their positions as groups. Why this regional difference? I would guess this is part of a continuing incremental realignment of grassroots politics in the South. Republican success in a presidential election has a clearer effect on minority Democratic turnover.

Clearly, one cannot assume that these Democrats are displaced by Republicans, especially in the southern "black belt."

It is extremely difficult to assert differences within the Republican Party. Of course, in light of Democratic differences, one might leap at the opportunity to find significance in turnover variations, which may be anomalous. If I accept the data as "hard," then there are differences within the Republican Party. The pattern for other male and female Republicans, North and South, is similar — a decline in turnover in 1984 and increase in turnover in the 1986 election. In the North, the 1986 turnover is less than the turnover in 1982, but in the South, there is greater turnover among other Republican females and less among males. If there are differences between white and Hispanic Republicans, the pattern of turnover in both regions increases during 1984 and declines in 1986 (again, note the extremely small percentages).

EXPLAINING DEMOCRATIC TURNOVER

The variables of this study explain 31 percent of the variance for all Democratic turnover during this time frame, but they explain somewhat more variance for each Democratic group: 35 percent for other females, 40 percent for blacks, and 62 percent for Hispanics. This explanatory variation suggests that any study of turnover must take into account different political environments. For example, the importance of multimember districts in increasing turnover only affects blacks, and it should be remembered that black representation was predicted by multi-member districts, at least in the South. These districts also predict total Republican turnover as well, but not the minority groups we are studying. In reality, turnover among our groups is likely to occur where their representation is already significant, and, because these constituencies differ, patterns of turnover will vary from group to group.

Table 4.6 addresses turnover among Democrats. Four variables strongly predict turnover among all Democrats whereas four others are marginal. Democrats have long been identified with traditional party organization states, and these states most strongly predict their turnover (*beta* .51). However, this variable is not the most important predictor of our minority groups in the Democratic Party. In fact, it is of secondary importance to females (*beta* .34), and it does not significantly predict black or Hispanic turnover. This is to be expected, I believe, because weak local Democratic organizations do not predict their representation, and traditional Democratic organizations simply do not perform the important roles in politics that they once did.

TABLE 4.6
Multiple Regression Analyses' *Betas* **of Democratic Groups'**
Turnover, in Three Elections

Independent Variables	All	Female	Black	Hispanic
Traditional Party				
Orgn. States	.51 a	.34 b	−.07 NS	.04 NS
Reduce Chambers	.16 d	.09 NS	.16 c	.01 NS
Hispanic Population	.26 b	−.36 b	.18 NS	.75 a
Cons. Protestants	−.33 b	−.42 a	.01 NS	−.05 NS
Committee Chairs	.28 b	.11 NS	.06 NS	.04 NS
Changed to Republican	.26 b	.09 NS	.03 NS	−.02 NS
Legislative Salary	−.22 d	−.30 d	.12 NS	.04 NS
Black Population	−.08 NS	−.24 d	.54 a	−.06 NS
Multimember District	.04 NS	−.08 NS	.23 c	−.10 NS
Metropolitan Population	.02 NS	−.15 NS	.26 c	−.01 NS
Education 16 + Years	.01 NS	.25 c	−.16 NS	.13 NS
Roman Catholic	.06 NS	−.24 d	.03 NS	−.04 NS
District Size	.08 NS	.09 NS	−.18 NS	−.40 a
R square	.31	.35	.40	.62

Notes: a = sig. < .001; b = sig. < .01; c = sig. < .05; d = sig. < .10; NS = not significant.

Traditionally, in the South at least, conservative Protestants as a percentage of state populations, must be considered Democratic voters in state legislative elections. I believe this fact should skew this analysis to some degree. The regression analysis indicates that the smaller the conservative Protestant population, the greater the turnover (*beta* .33) among Democrats. This dovetails well with the effect of traditional party organizations, largely in the metropolitan states of the North. During the 1980s, Democratic turnover was not very large in these southern, conservative Protestant states. This is at odds with the significant shifts in voting behavior toward the Republican Party in the presidential elections of this decade, not to mention the shifts between both parties in U.S. Senate elections. It would appear that the Democratic Party is holding its own at the grassroots level, and this is also true of Democratic females. Although the negative relationship indicates there is more turnover among females where there are fewer conservative Protestants (*beta* −.42), one must recognize there are few Democratic females in southern states, and this percentage has been declining during this time frame. My interpretation of this fact must be different. Democratic female turnover largely occurs in the North where their representation is much greater.

The percentage of conservative Protestants does not have a significant effect on blacks or Hispanics. Blacks have extensive representation in the North and South, and, although their turnover is slightly greater in the South, the small percentages do not effect a significant relationship.

Two variables associated with state legislatures — salaries (as a ratio of state per capita income) and committee chairs (as a proportion of chamber membership) — also predict Democratic turnover. Legislative salaries marginally function as expected (*beta* −.22, sig. < .10), that is, the smaller the salary ratio (smaller the difference between salary and per capita income), the greater the turnover. I think we can safely infer that fewer incentives exist to remain in the legislature if the remunerative benefits are small. Among our minority groups this variable more significantly predicts female turnover (*beta* −.30) but has no significant impact on black or Hispanic turnover. I think one may safely infer that the impoverishment of the black and Hispanic communities, not reflected in state per capita income, may mean that these salaries represent an incentive to remain in legislative office.

If legislative salaries function as expected, the committee chairs ratio does not fulfill expectations. A large proportion of chairs within a chamber does not provide incentives to remain in office. On the contrary, turnover is greater among Democrats (*beta* .28) where the ratio is greater. However, the variable does not predict female, black, or Hispanic turnover. One may infer that other males' turnover can be predicted by this variable.

The impact of political change from Democratic to Republican Party control affects, as expected, general Democratic turnover (*beta* .26). However, this change has no significant impact on females, blacks, or Hispanics. One is left with the conclusion that other Democratic males are the major losers during a change in legislative political control. It is intriguing that our three minority groups remain isolated from this political event. Blacks and Hispanics represent overwhelmingly safe Democratic districts. Even if Republicans take control of a legislative chamber, they are unlikely to take seats in black or Hispanic districts. It is intriguing that other Democratic females have been successful in escaping the effect of changed political control. One may posit that they may be better established as incumbents in their districts because it took so much hard work to overcome gender stereotypes to win their seats. Or, if they enter the legislature at a later age than males, their chances for upward mobility are not as great. Perhaps, they cannot leave the legislature as easily to start over. Whatever the reason, their success in achieving parity with Republican females may be due to this ability to remain in office. One can stipulate this fact because Republican female turnover is predicted by a change from Republican to Democratic control of legislative chambers (see discussion of Republican turnover below).

The reduction of the Illinois General Assembly during the early 1980s has also had a marginally significant impact on the Democratic Party (*beta* .26, sig. < .10). The only minority group whose turnover was affected proved to be blacks (*beta* .16). The assembly's reduction also meant that Illinois would move from multimember to single-member districts. It would appear the earlier multimember district system positively affected black representation because the change predicted only black, not Hispanic or female, turnover. Indeed, multimember districts, although not significant for general Democratic, female, or Hispanic turnover, do predict black turnover (*beta* .23).

A state's percentage of Hispanic population represents a final, marginal predictor of general Democratic turnover (*beta* −.23, sig. < .10). This turnover is likely to be greater where this population is small; in fact, this is also true of female turnover (*beta* −.36). However, the Hispanic population strongly and positively predicts Hispanic turnover (*beta* .75), a conclusion one could have reached without a sophisticated analysis. Although this may be true, it should also be noted that the size of legislative districts in terms of voting age population also predicts Hispanic turnover. This turnover is greater when the districts are smaller (*beta* −.40), and I think I am correct when I suggest that this is probably due to New Mexico where there is a very substantial Hispanic community. They have done very well in the legislature, and I think that this has skewed the results of this analysis.

The analyses in Tables 4.6 and 4.7 indicate a far richer analysis of turnover by party and attendant minority groups. If one simply assessed turnover that occurs within the Democratic Party, one would not have found that multimember districts and size of legislative districts predict only black and Hispanic turnover, respectively (noted above). One would also find that the proportion of blacks in a state had no significance to Democratic turnover, but this analysis indicates that where there are fewer blacks (*beta* −.24, sig. < .10), there will be greater female turnover. A larger proportion of blacks, however, significantly predicts black turnover (*beta* .54), as one might expect. There is no significant relationship with the Hispanic population.

Three factors that were important to representation — state metropolitan attributes, highly educated population (16 or more years of
education), and the percentage of Roman Catholics — only significantly
predict black or female turnover. Metropolitan attributes significantly
predict black turnover (*beta* .23), as one might expect, but not female or
Hispanic turnover. Female turnover is greatest when a state population is
highly educated, which is somewhat surprising. I had assumed females
would actually do well in states with an extremely high level of
education. Using this indicator they do not. Their representation tends to
be greater where the level of education is lower, and their turnover is
grater where the population is highly educated. Finally, female turnover
is greater where the percentage of Roman Catholics tends to be smaller
(*beta* .24, sig. < .10). This is a marginal predictor, but certainly important. It does not mean that large Catholic populations tend to reelect
females in large numbers; females do not obtain great representation in
those states. This is the same interpretation one would establish for the
effect of conservative Protestants on Democratic female representation.

TABLE 4.7
Multiple Regression Analyses' *Betas* of Republican Groups'
Turnover, in Three Elections

Independent Variables	All	Female	Hispanic
1984 Election	−.25 a	−.09 NS	−.09 NS
Multimember District	.29 a	.16 NS	.01 NS
Changed to Democrats	.33 a	.32 a	−.04 NS
Roman Catholic	.32 a	−.21 d	−.07 NS
Local Democratic Orgns.	−.24 b	−.15 NS	−.13 NS
Black Population	−.22 c	−.20 NS	.06 NS
Hispanic Population	.22 c	−.02 NS	.66 a
Changed to Republican	−.13 c	−.13 d	.05 NS
Cons. Protestants	.15 d	−.05 NS	−.12 NS
Traditional Party Orgn. States	.30 c	.09 NS	.03 NS
Discrimination	.01 NS	−.24 d	.05 NS
Females Employed	.12 NS	.23 d	−.12 NS
Committee Chairs	−.10 NS	−.18 d	−.04 NS
District Size	−.13 d	.12 NS	−.04 NS
R square	.69	.37	.39

Notes: a = sig. < .001; b = sig. < .01; c = sig. < .05; d = sig. < .10; NS = not
significant.

EXPLAINING REPUBLICAN TURNOVER

The regression analysis in Table 4.7 of general Republican turnover explains a robust 69 percent of the variance. Of the 22 variables used in this study, 11 are significant or marginally predict Republican turnover. However, only five of these variables help predict Republican female and Hispanic turnover. Three other independent variables aid in the explanation of female turnover, but not general Republican or Hispanic turnover. The variance explained by these regression analyses is 37 percent for females and 39 percent for Hispanics. Although certainly not as robust as the explanation of general Republican turnover analysis, each of these R squares is comparable to the national analysis, found in Chapter 2, of their representation within chambers.

It is interesting to note the varied importance of these independent variables for general Republican turnover and for the female and Hispanic minorities. For Republicans generally, turnover is likely to be greater in the 1982 reapportionment/recession-affected elections and in the 1986 off-year elections. The success of the Republican Party in the presidential election sharply decreases turnover (*beta* −.25), and as indicated in Table 4.1, has no other effect than this. Even Democratic turnover decreased during this election year, but not as dramatically. What is intriguing is that the presidential election has no comparable effect on females or Hispanics. This may be due in part to the small percentage of chambers' membership each represents. In any case, I think that if Republican turnover is significantly predicted by a number of variables that do not predict Republican minority turnover, then we may assume the significant impact is experienced by other Republican males (mostly white).

As indicated earlier, multimember districts do have a significant effect for Republican turnover (*beta* .29), but once again there is no significant impact on females or Hispanics. Niemi and Winsky indicate turnover in the United States is more likely to occur in states with multimember districts, perhaps due to the larger costs of running in these districts.[3] But by appraising turnover within parties and respective minority groups, it is clear that Republicans are affected, but not all Democrats, and certainly not females or Hispanics. This may be due to the relative success of both groups in metropolitan states where few multimember district systems exist.

One would expect Roman Catholic (*beta* .32) and conservative Protestant (*beta* .15, sig. < .10) religions to have a significant impact on Republican turnover. In the literature of political parties, Roman Catholics (with the exception of Cubans) and conservative Protestants in the

South have traditionally supported the Democratic Party. They still do in most state and local elections, and for this reason, Republican turnover tends to be greater where these populations are greater. However, conservative Protestantism does not significantly predict female or Hispanic turnover in the Republican Party. For females this might be explained by their growing success in the South. Cuban-Americans in Florida, while Roman Catholic, reside in a state that is far more Protestant than other northern states. However, the relationship between Roman Catholicism and female turnover is reversed; a negative, marginal predictor (*beta* −.21, sig. < .10). States with fewer Roman Catholics are likely to sustain greater female turnover.

Party factors also play a vital role in explaining Republican turnover. Republican turnover is reasonably more likely to be greater where local Democratic organizations are quite strong (*beta* −.24) and in traditional party organization states, which are likely to be Democratic (*beta* .30). In these states, one would expect that Democrats are more capable of marshaling electoral resources to challenge Republican incumbents. Competitive seats, where they exist, probably strain incumbent resources to the point that representatives look to other public offices or the private sector for safer employment. Neither of these party variables predicts female or Hispanic turnover, although a clear, but insignificant, negative relationship exists for females.

One would also expect that a change in party fortunes in the control of legislative chambers would have some effect on turnover. When a legislative chamber becomes Democratic, Republican turnover is likely to increase (*beta* .33). There is, however, no significant impact on Hispanics who are isolated from these effects. Females are significantly affected by a change in chamber control unlike their Democratic peers who seem to be isolated from changes to Republican control (Table 4.6). I think this represents one factor associated with the present parity between Democratic and Republican females in the 1980s. Similarly, one would expect that changes to Republican control would significantly decrease (*beta* −.13) general Republican turnover. Females are also marginally affected (*beta* −.13, sig. < .10).

Hispanic turnover is not significantly affected by a change to Republican control. Of course, the largest group of successful Republican Hispanics is in Florida. The lower chamber remains Democratic there although these majorities have consistently declined each of these election years. One may simply state that the same factors predicting Democratic Hispanic turnover also predict Republican Hispanic turnover: a large percent of the population is Hispanic (*beta* .66) and the size of districts in terms of voting age population (*beta* –.31). The presence of a Hispanic population also predicts general Republican turnover (*beta* .22), but it has no significant impact on women. Generally, Hispanic Republican turnover is occurring where the districts are quite small in terms of voting age populations.

This latter variable also has a marginal effect on general Republican turnover (*beta* –.13, sig. < .10), but not on Republican women. It is interesting to note that although the *beta* is not significant for females, it is clearly positive, that is, larger districts may have some impact on their turnover. Additionally, general Republican turnover is predicted in states where the black population is smaller (*beta* –.22), but this simply indicates that Republicans are not likely to be found in states with very large black populations, especially in the South. In other words, you cannot have turnover where you are not represented.

I think this relationship may change, especially if the election rules associated with southern primaries are successfully challenged in federal courts. In the multiple, statewide candidate primaries, one candidate must obtain a clear majority, or there is a runoff in which a black candidate is likely to lose. It has been the Republican administration's Justice Department view to protect black representatives, not only for purposes of civil rights, but also to identify the Democratic Party as a party of black politicians. This policy has driven whites (North and South) into the Republican Party in presidential elections. The effect of overturning the southern primary system is likely to accelerate the realignment of southern politics at the state and local levels. If that is the case, this *beta*'s direction could change.

The fragmentation of the Democratic Party in large part explains the success of the Republican Party since 1968, but nowhere in this study do local Republican organizations have a significant impact. This suggests that Republicans have not yet built significant local organizations or simply that, with media and new election technology, the "image" one seeks to portray has become central to Republican success. Where Republicans have greater turnover, local Democratic organizations are strong. In this sense, local party organizations are still viable in the mediacracy age.

Three remaining independent variables significantly predict only female Republican success: the discrimination index (*beta* –.24, sig. < .10), percent of females employed (*beta* .23, sig. < .10), and the proportion of committee chairs to the number of chamber members (*beta* –.18, sig. < .10). Each of these variables is marginally significant and represents some interesting relationships in states that must be quite volatile for women candidates. Republican women are found in states that have earlier passed legislation affecting political and economic discrimination and where more women were employed. They are also likely to suffer greater turnover in these states. Women are also likely to experience greater turnover when there are fewer committee chairs as a proportion of a chamber's membership. Fewer committees, in my opinion, may reflect better organization in terms of specialization and accountability, but fewer committees also represent fewer positions of power over policy. Perhaps this relationship reflects this latter fact. Because of fewer opportunities to affect policy as a chairperson, females experience frustration and leave the legislature. It is unlikely that they are defeated for office because incumbency also works effectively for them.

The evidence indicates that one cannot simply appraise turnover among legislators. One must differentiate by party membership and, I would strongly add, the varied groups that represent parties in legislatures. There is an increased richness to be found in such analysis, although some ambiguities inevitably remain in correlational analyses using state data bases.

NOTES

1. Richard Niemi and Laura R. Winsky, "Membership Turnover in U.S. State Legislatures: Trends and Effects of Districting," *Legislative Studies Quarterly* 12 (February 1987): 115–23; Kwang S. Shinn and John S. Jackson III, "Membership Turnover in U.S. State Legislatures: 1931–1976," *Legislative Studies Quarterly* 4 (February 1979): 95–104; Alan Rosenthal, "Turnover in State Legislatures," *American Journal of Political Science* 18 (1974): 606–16; Dianne Kincaid and Ann R. Henry, "The Family Factor in State Legislative Turnover," *Legislative Studies Quarterly* 6 (1981): 55–68; Emily Stoper, "Wife and Politician: Role Strain among Women in Public Office," in Marianne Githens and Jewell S. Prestage, eds., *A Portrait of Marginality* (New York: David McKay, 1977). One should note that neither the Niemi and Winsky nor the Shinn and Jackson study sought to differentiate turnover by party attachment, minority groups, or gender.

2. See the work of John F. Bibby, "Patterns of Midterm Gubernatorial and State Legislative Elections," *Public Opinion Quarterly* 6 (1983): 41–46; James E. Campbell, "Presidential Coattails and Midterm Losses in State Legislative Elections," *American Political Science Review* 80 (March 1986): 45–64.

3. Niemi and Winsky, "Membership Turnover."

5

MINORITY INFLUENCE AND POLICY EFFECTS

Thus far, I have assessed incorporation as a process including representation affected by the incidence of minority turnover in state legislatures. These are important factors, but one more step in the process of incorporation is essential. Minorities, to be effective, must occupy positions of influence within legislative chambers. They must become party leaders or committee chairpersons. In doing so they will obtain greater control of a chamber's political agenda and have a greater effect on policy making.

After minorities achieve positions of authority, one may expect minority policy preferences to be written into law, if, and this is extremely important, they are members of the dominant party. The control of a chamber's agenda and policy substance is largely determined by the majority party, although divided government ought to increase partisan compromise of policy preferences. For this reason, it is very difficult to suggest that, for example, "women's representation" or "Hispanic representation" should predict certain policy outcomes. Because Democratic women have recently achieved parity with their sisters, it also means that they have increased their representation within their party. Their position within a majority party also enhances their policy influence. Unfortunately for Republican women and Hispanics, the Democratic Party controls most of the legislative chambers in this study. Republicans are likely to be left out in the cold, but ideally, black, Hispanic, and other female Democrats' representation within their party should predict their political influence as committee chairs and party leaders. This is not the only reason to differentiate minorities by party. Minority Democrats and Republicans may have the same societal goals, but they may disagree about the means to these ends. These means represent the essence of policy conflict over valued goals.

AN INDEX OF POTENTIAL INFLUENCE

The influence of minority members will be based on the construction of "potential influence" indices. These values are associated with different party and committee leadership positions found in the Council of State Governments' publications.[1] Unlike an earlier analysis in 1987, it takes into account majority and minority party differences.[2] The choice of values was made in consultation with other political scientists with very little unanimity among them. Clearly, the highest values should be associated with majority party leaders and chairs of the fiscal policy committees. These rankings are based on the impact they have on public policy and the legislative agenda. High values are also associated with the Rules and Judiciary Committees because they also concern the legislative agenda and laws governing the states. In addition, I have placed moderately high values on business committees because business does have a privileged position as part of "distributive coalitions" that have an important impact on national and state economies.[3] The remaining values recognize the importance of committee chairs who are "often the committee" or who share power with a small group of interested members who may dominate committee proceedings.[4]

The potential influence indices reported are quite simple to calculate for each minority group. I intend to produce proportional indices of influence based on each group's influence found in parties and as chairs of the committee system.

The result of this calculation may be properly termed a proportion, but I hesitate to be so precise; therefore, the indices are simply referred to as "potential influence" — and for good reason. Caution must be suggested in the use of these indices because legislatures vary in terms of their professionalism, functions, and influence within their respective states. In fact, reporting these indices may be misleading because most states do not list or have ranking minority members on committees. In many southern states, no minority leadership structure exists, or the minority party's leadership may not be fully reported. In many respects this reflects the importance of the majority party in policy making. But, in spite of these difficulties, the indices represent a legitimate attempt to go beyond simple proportions of a group's representation in state legislatures. I seek to ascertain how much potential influence each group may have over the legislative agenda from 1983 to 1987 as party leaders and committee officers.

Three concerns must be addressed to assess fully successful incorporation. First, what potential influence does each minority group hold following the three elections in this study? Does each group's representation translate into political influence within legislative chambers? And finally, does this influence significantly predict policy outcomes? If representation translates into "club" membership and impact on policy outcomes, one might stipulate that the political system is responsive.

Using Table 5.1, I create two indices associated with my first concern, what influence each minority group may hold. The first represents the proportion of influence minorities have in their respective parties. Do they hold positions such as Speaker of the House, Caucus Chair, Majority Leader, or other leadership positions? If so, their potential influence represents the sum of the values associated with position held, divided by the total sum of party leadership values.[5]

The second index includes the varied values of committee chairs held by minority members. The sum of these values is added to the party leadership score and divided by the total values of reported party and committee leadership positions. It is clear that female, black, and Hispanic influence is a function of belonging to a chamber's majority party. Obviously, this does not enhance the influence of a Republican minority, whose party controlled 11 chambers in 1983, 15 in 1985, and 13 in 1987. Whether a Republican minority member sponsors legislation or not may indicate only policy interest, not influence.

TABLE 5.1
Index Values Associated with Party Leadership and Committee Chair Positions

Majority Leaders	Values	Minority Leadership
Speaker of House	10	—
Caucus Chair, Majority Leader, Speaker Pro Tem	9	—
Chairs, Fiscal Policy	8	Minority Leader
Chairs, Rules, Judiciary	7	Ranking Members of Fiscal Policy
Other Party Leaders	6	Ranking Rules, Judiciary Members
Chairs, Business & Labor	5	Other Party Leaders
Chairs, Other Committees	4	Ranking, Business Members
	3	Ranking, Other Committees

My second concern addresses the effects of representation. Does it translate into "club" membership? The influence of women, blacks, and Hispanics varies. Is this variation a function of representation within their respective parties? If so, the effect on policy outcomes is assumed, my third major concern. I expect that each minority group, regardless of party membership (although a Republican minority member is disadvantaged), has a significant impact on programs associated with Human Resources (per capita expenditures for education, social services, and mental health/hospitals). Female interest is predicated on patterns of socialization emphasizing "care-oriented" roles in our culture. Often an issue concerning prenatal care, childcare, teen pregnancy, education, social services and their reform, civil rights, and a host of similar issues is narrowly defined as a woman's issue. This is in keeping with the cultural stereotype, but this is too narrow a definition. Each of these issues will also be a serious concern to a black or Hispanic representing an impoverished central city or, in the case of many southern blacks, a rural constituency. Each of these representatives is likely to be as "liberal" as other women based on constituent needs.[6]

My analysis is divided into three sections. The first is a comparison of each group's potential influence within each party using simple descriptive statistics. Once the influence of each group is ascertained, a second section ascertains whether representation within parties does predict influence in parties and total leadership influence (party and committee chairs). I report bivariate regression analyses' multiple Rs and R squares to determine the variance explained by party representation. Finally, first-order partial correlation coefficients are used to ascertain whether the total potential influence of each group predicts three human resource per capita expenditures while controlling for per capita income: education, social services, and mental health/hospitals.

POTENTIAL INFLUENCE IN CHAMBERS

The Democrats

The appraisal of influence within chambers must necessarily include the dominant players — other Democratic males — for purposes of comparison to ascertain how well each group is doing in the struggle for influence. Greater power is associated with each Democratic group if it controls chambers or shares power in divided chambers. I would not expect each of these Democratic groups to be very influential in chambers controlled by the Republican Party.

Table 5.2 indicates the proportion of influence within the Democratic Party for males and females (other than blacks and Hispanics), blacks and Hispanics. The table indicates that male influence in chambers controlled by the Democratic Party is extremely stable. In fact, it has increased slightly from 81.8 percent in 1983 to 82.6 percent in 1987. Their influence within chambers controlled by the Republican Party sharply declines from 92.7 percent to 81.2 percent during the same years. One might be cynical and suggest that there is little influence to be gained in these positions, hence a lack of interest. In chambers where there is a partisan split, power is more dispersed, and male influence is considerably lower — in the mid-70 percentile range. This is much closer to their average representation within their party, about 75 percent (see Table 3.1 in Chapter 3). Apparently the division between parties creates a situation where minority groups will obtain greater influence to retain their support. (One must be very cautious because there are very few partisan split chambers.)

TABLE 5.2

Democratic Groups' Proportion of Potential Influence in Their Party, by Chamber Control and Year

(in percent)

	Years		
Groups & Chamber Control	1983	1985	1987
Males*			
Democratic	81.8	83.1	82.6
Republican	92.7	87.8	81.2
Split Control	—	74.0	76.0
Females*			
Democratic	8.3	8.7	10.7
Republican	3.9	7.4	17.5
Split Control	—	10.0	24.0
Blacks			
Democratic	8.0	6.5	4.3
Republican	0.0	0.5	0.0
Split Control	—	0.0	0.0
Hispanics			
Democratic	2.0	1.2	2.1
Republican	2.6	3.7	0.0
Split Control	—	16.0	0.0

*Other than blacks and Hispanics.

Women's (other than blacks and Hispanics) influence within Democratically controlled chambers has slowly increased from 8.3 percent in 1983 to 10.7 percent in 1987. This still represents influence that does not reach parity with female representation within their party, about 15 percent. The largest increase in influence actually occurs between 1985 and 1987, although it would be inappropriate to stipulate that a 2 percent gain represents a sharp increase in political influence. However, their influence does sharply increase from 3.9 percent in 1983 to 17.5 percent in chambers controlled by the Republican Party. Female influence is also greater in chambers where there is a split in partisan control.

Although female Democratic influence has sharply increased in chambers where the Republican Party is dominant, control of a Republican chamber's agenda is unlikely to be the result of Democratic initiatives. Within chambers that are split between parties, their influence is much more meaningful. In 1985 and 1987, their influence was 10 percent and 24 percent, respectively. In this situation, I think it appropriate to suggest that women have greater influence because it is necessary to retain their support within the legislature and with the voters. In a party system that performs systemic integration, the symbolic or substantive recognition of groups may encourage greater support in the next election. If this succeeds, then a party is likely to be successful in the forthcoming election.

Among blacks in the Democratic Party, there has only been a continuous decline in potential influence by approximately one-half, from 8.0 percent in 1983 to 4.3 percent in 1987. Although black influence is closely tied to representation within the Democratic Party in 1983, this influence falls to approximately 66 percent of their representation in 1987. Blacks are overwhelmingly Democratic, but the reward for voting thus has obtained diminished returns. I interpret this, rather cynically, to be an attempt to remove blacks from visible positions of power in order to counter the image of a black Democratic Party. Increased black political activism in the 1980s has been successfully used in Republican campaigns to suggest that the Democratic Party may no longer represent the interests of white, middle-class ethnics. There is another possible explanation. One may also view this as a continuing political conflict at the state level to redress black political influence in the cities, particularly because many state governments do not care to take responsibility for urban problems.

There are few blacks in states whose chambers are controlled by Republicans or where chamber control is split. Whether blacks would obtain greater influence in either case is difficult to ascertain. I would think that if there were a more competitive environment, blacks would also increase their influence in their party's councils.

Finally, Hispanic influence remains quite stable at about 2 percent in chambers controlled by the Democratic Party. This represents influence that is slightly less than their representation within the party. It is slightly higher, much like female influence, in chambers controlled by the Republican Party (2.6 percent in 1983 rising to 3.7 percent in 1985, no influence in 1987). In a chamber where partisan control was split (1985), the group's influence was 16 percent, far greater than one would expect.

Total Democratic influence (including party and committee chairs) mirrors similar patterns in the dispersion of influence (see Table 5.3). Male influence remains quite stable between 83 percent and 84 percent in Democratically controlled chambers during each year. This is somewhat, but not significantly, greater than the influence held in party leadership

TABLE 5.3

Democratic Groups' Proportion of Total Potential Influence as Party Leaders and Committee Chairpersons, by Chamber Control and Year

(in percent)

| Groups & Chamber Control | Years | | |
	1983	1985	1987
Males*			
Democratic	84.0	83.9	83.4
Republican	91.1	88.5	81.7
Split Control	—	74.0	82.0
Females*			
Democratic	8.5	8.6	10.5
Republican	5.6	6.7	16.8
Split Control	—	19.0	18.0
Blacks			
Democratic	5.5	5.9	4.4
Republican	0.0	0.5	0.0
Split Control	—	0.0	0.0
Hispanics			
Democratic	1.9	1.8	1.7
Republican	2.6	3.7	0.0
Split Control	—	9.0	0.0

*Other than blacks and Hispanics.

posts. Where Republicans control chambers, total male influence also sharply declines from 91.1 percent in 1983 to 81.7 percent in 1987. When there is a partisan split in a legislature, their potential influence is clearly lower in 1983 (74.0). But in 1987, it would appear that much male influence is retrieved through the control of committee chairs (82 percent). This represents influence nearly equal to that found in Democratically controlled chambers.

Female total potential influence mildly increases in Democratically controlled chambers from 8.5 percent in 1983 to 10.5 percent in 1987. It appears that females have not obtained increased influence as committee chairs because there is little variation between the total and party influence indices. However, their influence sharply increases in chambers controlled by Republicans, but at levels somewhat below their party success. In part this is due to some states reporting ranking minority members in committee systems or dispersing chairs to minority party members. Finally, female influence is significantly greater in chambers where there is a partisan split, although the 18.0 percent influence in 1987 is less than the proportion of influence (24.0 percent) obtained within their party in the same chambers. This decline may simply indicate that the number of women was not great enough to also hold additional chairs.

Total black influence is more erratic when one adds the control of party chairs. Over the entire period, their influence declines by 20 percent, but it is obvious the 5.5 percent index in 1983 suggests that they held a lower proportion of committee chairs. In 1985, this total influence increases to 5.9 percent suggesting a small increase in the control of party chairs, but a serious decline in party influence. Black influence falls to 4.4 percent indicating that they control a similar proportion of party and committee power. This loss was obtained in each political arena.

Hispanic total influence remains stable although some differences do exist in all types of chambers. Their influence is approximately 2 percent in Democratic chambers, is somewhat greater in Republican-controlled chambers, and, finally, is greater in a partisan split chamber. One should be aware that the influence held in this political arena represents less (total of 9 percent) influence than Hispanics held in party leadership positions in 1985.

The Republicans

Influence is less dispersed in the Republican Party's leadership roles, particularly to Republican females. Republican women have long outnumbered their counterparts in the Democratic Party, but, as Table 5.4

TABLE 5.4
Republican Groups' Proportion of Potential Influence in Their Party, by Chamber Control and Year
(in percent)

		Years	
Groups & Chamber Control	1983	1985	1987
Males*			
Democratic	89.7	85.7	81.7
Republican	90.4	87.9	91.2
Split Control	—	72.0	100.0
Females*			
Democratic	9.7	13.1	18.1
Republican	9.0	11.6	8.2
Split Control	—	0.0	0.0
Hispanics			
Democratic	0.0	0.8	0.0
Republican	0.0	0.0	0.0
Split Control	—	28.0	0.0

*Other than Hispanics.

indicates, within Republican controlled chambers, their party influence rises and falls.

Male influence remains quite high in party leadership positions with a dip in potential influence in 1985. In Republican chambers, males do better than their Democratic peers controlling between 90 percent and 91 percent of party influence in 1983 and 1987. This is well above their representation of 81 percent to 83 percent in the Republican Party. With no explanation, male influence declines to 87.9 percent, but it still is greater than Democratic male influence in any year. Republican male influence does decline from approximately 90 percent in 1983 to 82 percent in 1987 in chambers controlled by Democrats. This is similar to the pattern found in the Democratic Party and is expected. There is little control of a chamber's agenda to be found in Democratically controlled chambers.

In this environment, it is not surprising that female influence in the party increases when control of the chamber's agenda is at best minimal. Past empirical evidence has indicated that women's political presence was more likely if less influence was attached to an office. Female influence rises from 9.7 percent in 1983 (well above the influence of Democratic females in the same position) to 18.1 percent in 1987 (about the same influence for Democratic females in a similar environment). However, in chambers controlled by their party, their influence is erratic and does not continually increase. Female representation within their party is about 17 percent, but the influence they obtain is approximately one-half of this. In fact, female influence is less in 1987 than it was in 1983. Initially, their influence within the Republican Party stood at 9.0 percent and rose to 11.6 percent in 1985 then declined in 1987 to 8.2 percent, well below the influence held by Democratic women in their party. There is no clear explanation for this other than the fact that Republican representation did fall after the 1986 election (see Chapter 4). Unlike Democratic women in chambers split between the parties, Republican women have no leadership positions within their own party.

It is not really possible to assess Republican Hispanic success. Cuban-American voters live in New York and especially Florida, but these states' legislative chambers are controlled by the Democratic Party. This means their influence is further minimized in the committee system where they will have absolutely no representation. In Florida, one also has a traditionalistic culture that is less amenable to minority recognition, although the governor is Hispanic. Perhaps legislative influence may be shared with Hispanics in the future. In New York, the percentage of Cuban-American voters is quite small and unlikely to be reflected in any aspect of incorporation.

Table 5.5 indicates that the total male influence in Republican chambers is somewhat less than the proportion of influence obtained in party leadership positions. This indicates that political influence is more widely dispersed in the committee system and that the major beneficiaries are women, not Hispanics whose representation in the party is minimal.

Although total male influence is somewhat less than the influence held in party posts, males clearly have greater political influence in legislatures controlled by their party; 88.7 percent in 1983, 84.1 percent in 1985, and 86.5 percent in 1987. Males have given up more influence in Democratic chambers, from 92.4 percent to 81.7 percent in 1983 and 1987, respectively. I think the importance of an office affects its desirability, and the competition for the post is likely to increase. If little power is attached to the post, less influential members (women in this study) of the party are likely to obtain them.

Republican women's influence rises significantly in chambers controlled by their party, from 11.3 percent in 1983 to 15.9 percent in 1985. This means women's influence within legislative chambers has reached parity associated with their party representation of approximately 16

TABLE 5.5

Republican Groups' Total Potential Influence as Party Leaders and Committee Chairpersons, by Chamber Control and Year (in percent)

Groups & Chamber Control	Years		
	1983	*1985*	*1987*
Males*			
Democratic	92.4	83.5	81.7
Republican	88.7	84.1	86.5
Split Control	—	78.0	100.0
Females*			
Democratic	6.9	16.8	11.1
Republican	11.3	15.9	12.8
Split Control	—	0.0	0.0
Hispanics			
Democratic	0.0	1.7	0.0
Republican	0.0	0.0	0.6
Split Control	—	22.0	0.0

*Other than Hispanics.

percent. However, the decline in the number of chambers controlled by the Republican Party from 15 to 11 in 1987 has also sharply reduced women's influence to 12.8 percent, well below their 17 percent representation in the Republican Party. Such a loss could represent a short-term anomaly to be made up in the future.

Their representation in chambers controlled by Democrats shows a sharp increase from 6.9 percent in 1983 to 16.8 percent in 1985. This increase is much like that of Democratic women in Republican chambers. But the similarity stops there when it drops to 11.1 percent in 1987. Once again, is this an anomalous data point, or does it represent a real decline in legislative influence? Because little influence really rests with the minority party, it is likely that women's influence within these Democratically controlled chambers will reach parity with their party representation. Perhaps, it will extend beyond representation because holding these posts may have little influence attached within chambers. Although they reflect very little legislative power, the posts held can be important to a wider public, represent symbolic recognition of women, and be important role models to other women who may have an interest in politics.

Hispanic representation is so minimal that it does not really translate into any significant influence, with the exception of one state where power is split between parties. In this state, Hispanic influence represents 22 percent of all Republican influence in the chamber. In 1987, their influence is 0.6 percent among the 11 chambers in Republican hands, and other than these two instances, Hispanic Republicans hold little influence in legislative chambers.

REPRESENTATION AND PARTY INFLUENCE

Representation in chambers is almost meaningless unless it can predict minority group influence. If it does, then one can make a case for a responsive political system. It should be remembered that political leaders in lower state legislative chambers have greater latitude in dispensing political offices. Representation may not predict leadership influence because of personal preferences that could either hinder or support minorities in legislative chambers. When representation does not predict influence, political leaders may think that the representation is not significant enough to reward with leadership positions. It is also possible that influence may outrun the contemporary significance of a minority group because of a group's future significance to state and, perhaps, national elections.

In this section, I report multiple R's and R squares from simple bivariate regression analyses in which minority representation within chambers is expected to predict influence in parties. It should also predict the sum of influence in parties and committee chair positions. The most important statistic is the R square, which represents the proportion of the variance explained. Ideally, the R squares should become greater as chambers respond to the representation and to demands for parity influence inside chambers.

Explaining Democratic Influence

In the tradition of U.S. politics, I would assume that minority influence would be the direct result of representation within their respective parties. At some point, this representation becomes significant to a party's political success. The minority group then gets the attention of political leaders who in turn provide political leadership posts. An assessment of R squares, associated with party leadership in Table 5.6, indicates that, with the exception of Hispanics, representation in the Democratic Party statistically explains less variance of party leadership

TABLE 5.6

Regression Analyses Predicting Democratic Groups' Total Potential Influence with Their Representation in the Democratic Party, by Year

| | Years and Influence | | | | | |
| | 1983 | | 1985 | | 1987 | |
Groups & Statistics	Party	Total	Party	Total	Party	Total
Males*						
Mult. R	.61	.68	.51	.64	.47	.67
R square	.37	.49	.26	.41	.22	.44
Females*						
Mult. R	.38	.45	.45	.69	.26	.52
R square	.15	.21	.21	.47	.07	.27
Blacks						
Mult. R	.59	.65	.51	.77	.44	.76
R square	.35	.43	.26	.59	.19	.57
Hispanics						
Mult. R	.90	.96	.94	.99	.91	.96
R square	.80	.92	.88	.98	.83	.92

*Other than blacks and Hispanics.

posts in 1987 than it does in 1983. This is contrary to expectations. The amplitude of these R squares also differs from group to group.

In 1983, the largest R square (.80) is related to Hispanic representation's explanation of party leadership. In part, the size of this statistic is related to the sensitivity of regression analysis to skewed data. The effect is largely associated with Hispanic success in New Mexico and, to a lesser extent, California. The fact that only a few states have a significant Hispanic population would enhance the effect of skewedness.

However, one must stipulate that attention is being paid to Hispanic representation. Hispanics will probably become the largest minority group in the country by the twenty-first century, and for this reason it is appropriate to recognize their importance. In providing them party leadership posts, there is an attempt to recruit the mass of Hispanic voters into the Democratic Party. Although this recruitment might reflect symbolic recognition of Hispanic importance, in New Mexico it is not symbolic. Hispanics carry out the important responsibilities of governance because they represent a substantial portion of the state's population and party representation. Their representation in the Democratic Party increasingly explains their influence in party posts, .88 in 1985 after the presidential election and .83 (R squares) in 1987.

Representation in the Democratic Party explains less of the influence obtained in the party among the remaining groups. Male (other than blacks and Hispanics) representation's ability to explain their proportion of leadership declines from 37 percent in 1983 to 22 percent. Their influence or representation has not generally decreased, but the pattern of apportioning influence within chambers may be more closely associated with personalities, varying chamber rules, traditions, and cultural values.

In Table 5.2, women and blacks find their influence in the Democratic Party going in different directions. While black influence has declined to about 60 percent of their representation in 1987, women's influence has slightly increased to approximately 70 percent of their representation in 1987. In both cases, their party representation explains less variance of their party leadership in 1987.

Black representation in the Democratic Party explains 35 percent of the variance associated with party leadership in 1983. It continues to gradually decline to 26 percent in 1985 and 19 percent in 1987. I would suggest that this decline in more visible positions of party influence may be planned. Although black representation declines somewhat in 1987, their influence in the party drops more quickly. Cynically, one might explain the decline of influence to an attempt to decrease black visibility in party leadership circles in order to maintain support with other members of the Democratic coalition. After all, in what way does the Republican Party present an alternative to their needs and interests? In a sense, blacks are captives in the two-party system and have no real option but to be Democrats. In this predicament, their influence can be subtly limited to have less effect on party councils addressing policy agendas.

It is more difficult to interpret the decline in variance explained by women's (other than blacks and Hispanics) party representation. Women's representation in the Democratic Party explained only 15 percent of the variance associated with their party leadership index, the lowest among the four groups, in 1983. This increased to 21 percent in 1985 and fell to an abysmal 7 percent in 1987. In fact, their party influence had actually increased, but this was obviously due to other factors: personality, varying chamber rules, traditions, and, perhaps, cultural values. Clearly, the Democratic Party was not responding to the reality of women's representation in all states. If one were interested in maintaining and increasing the support of women, representation should function to predict influence within the party. There may be another explanation for this statistical finding; where else can liberal women go, if not the Democratic Party? The Republican Party's conservatism is not an option. Perhaps a third party movement would be a viable alternative to their present plight. It would be interesting to note what proportion of third party candidates in local and state elections are women. In fact, the increasing visibility of the Green Party in different states may provide a response to women's interests and be a potential vehicle to obtain power in the future.

If the visible influence attached to party leadership is not predicted by party representation, total influence is better explained by party representation. Total influence includes the less visible, but equally important committee chairs. These chairpersons represent some of the most influential members of state legislatures. Often, chairpersons are the committee because members of a formal committee may find their attention divided among other committee appointments.[7]

The total influence index increases the proportion of variance explained by party leadership for every group. Among Hispanics, the proportion of variance explained by party representation is greater: 92 percent in 1983, 98 percent in 1985, and 92 percent in 1987. Once again I would caution the reader to recognize the effects of skewedness, which would exist in this analysis. And yet, it is quite clear that a response to Hispanic influence may be related to expectations of their potential influence in state and national politics. Whether this influence is translated into support for per capita policy expenditures would probably provide an answer to the quality of these findings.

The variance explained for Democratic women's total influence is greater than that explained for that found in their party. In 1983, their representation explains 21 percent of the variance associated with their total influence. This increases to 47 percent after the 1984 election but falls to 27 percent in 1987. In essence, women's representation by 1987 explains less of their influence in state legislative chambers. Other factors, such as personality, specific interests and skills, cultural values, and chamber traditions, have carried influence.

If this is particularly true of women, it is less true of the black experience in the legislature. Their influence does explain a large proportion of variance related to their total influence. While their representation explains less and less of the variance associated with party leadership, a greater proportion of their total influence is explained following the 1984 and 1986 elections. For example, in 1983, their representation explained 43 percent of their total influence. This is comparable to the explanation of other male influence, which was 49 percent during the same year. From this point on, black representation becomes even more important in explaining their total influence: 59 percent and 57 percent in 1985 and 1987, respectively. This research indicates that the explanation of other males' total influence is rather stable, 41 percent in 1985 and 44 percent in 1987. Of course, their influence is somewhat greater than their representation would indicate.

It is intriguing that Hispanic and black total influence should be a greater function of representation than that associated with other males and females. In U.S. politics, there is always some recognition of important party constituent groups. This research finds that there is an attempt to respond to minority representation and provide positions of influence within chambers. Earlier, I suggested that many in the Democratic Party are generally concerned about its being identified as a party of black constituents and leaders. For this reason, black influence among the more visible party leadership was decreased, and it is not as strongly associated with their representation. This is reversed within the committee system where a committee chair is less likely to be highly visible. Hispanic representation is strongly related to their influence in both the party and the committee system. Again, influence is obtained due to Hispanic influence within the Democratic coalition and on the basis of their future importance in U.S. politics.

For males and females that are generally Caucasian, representation is less important to the explanation of their influence. Other factors matter, and perhaps the greatest element is gender, which is blurred in the analysis of blacks and Hispanics. Clearly, female Democrats do not obtain their influence as a function of representation; the variance explained is too small. Custom, tradition, and, perhaps, cultural values associated with gender better explain the influence of Democratic women.

Explaining Republican Influence

The analysis of the effect of representation on influence indicates that Hispanic Republican representation is so small that it has no significant impact on influence in the Republican Party. Only other males and females (other than Hispanics) can be fruitfully analyzed. In Table 5.7, the influence of males and females is increasingly explained by the representation each has obtained. This is clearly different from the analysis of Democrats.

In 1983, female representation has absolutely no relationship (R square equals .00) to their influence within the Republican Party. However, their representation increasingly explains their influence in 1985 and 1987 — 22 percent and 26 percent of the variance explained

TABLE 5.7

Regression Analyses Predicting Republican Groups' Total Potential Influence with Their Representation in the Republican Party, by Year

	Years and Influence					
	1983		1985		1987	
Groups & Statistics	Party	Total	Party	Total	Party	Total
Males*						
Mult. R	.04	.41	.49	.63	.52	.66
R square	.001	.17	.24	.40	.27	.43
Females*						
Mult. R	.002	.49	.47	.63	.51	.68
R square	.00	.24	.22	.39	.26	.42
Hispanics**	—	—	—	—	—	—

*Other than Hispanics.
**No regression analysis possible.

respectively. It would appear that decisions on who obtains a leadership position in the party is becoming increasingly a function of representation. What is particularly important is that the explanation of Republican female party leadership now closely parallels the explanation of Democratic female success. This implies that both parties give similar weight to female representation in their ranks.

Among other Republican males, the variance explained increasingly is also a function of their representation. Male influence is not explained by representation in 1983 (R square equals .00 also), but it increasingly does explain male influence in 1985 (R square equals .24) and 1987 (R square equals .27). The increased importance of representation in apportioning influence within the Republican Party suggests a greater awareness of the importance of women to the party. Can this change be explained as an attempt to affect the gender gap in party identification and possible voting behavior? If the party's leaders increasingly tap females for leadership positions, each of the Republican Party's successes might be greater in future years. It would be interesting if in future years that representation was an increasingly important predictor of women's influence in the Republican Party. Although there is evidence of representation's increasing importance, one cannot be assured it will pass the .27 associated with Democratic females in 1987. In essence, I do not know if there is an absolute level beyond which female representation will not translate into greater political influence. After all, although there seems to be a more patterned response among the state legislatures to Republican female representation, female influence is actually less within the Republican Party in 1987 than it was in 1983 and in 1985 (see Table 5.4).

By adding committee chairs to the analysis of influence, it is quite obvious that representation becomes a more important explanation of both male and female influence in the Republican Party. Unfortunately, the multiple regression analyses of Hispanic Republican influence once again do not yield results, but the findings are more robust for males and females.

In 1983, Republican female representation explains 24 percent of the variance related to their total influence, compared to no variance explained related to their party influence. The variance explained continues to rise to 39 percent in 1985 and to 42 percent in 1987, and it is quite similar to the variance explained for other Republican males. Although the variance explained for males is significantly less in 1983 (17 percent), there is little difference in 1985 (40 percent) and 1987 (43 percent).

In fact, the white Democratic and Republican legislators' representation explains about 40 percent of the variance associated with their respective total influence in 1985 and 1987. However, the explanation of Democratic female influence in 1987 falls to 27 percent. It is unclear whether this is an anomalous event, particularly because the patterns of variance explained for the other three groups of largely white legislators are so similar.

EXPLAINING POLICY OUTCOMES

Three 1985 policy expenditures represent my dependent variables: per capita expenditures for education, social welfare, and mental health and hospitals. The choice of the three per capita policy expenditures is based on the likely policy preferences of minorities in this study. Generally, women are concerned with the dual roles they perform — work outside the home as well as adequate care for the family. One may expect policy concerns for social welfare services that might address prenatal care, day care needs, welfare reform, the feminization of poverty, teen pregnancy, and education. One might also expect strong concerns about mental health and hospital expenditures because there is a strong strain in our culture that says women are more likely to respond in a nurturing fashion. Each of these policy expenditures is associated with the liberal agenda discussed by Welch and others as women's issues.[8] Taking the position that these are women's issues would be narrow sighted. Clearly, these issues and expenditures would be important to the black and Hispanic communities, which need quality education, social services, and health care.

If representation significantly predicts total influence, does the total influence associated with each group predict support for each policy? I am assuming that the greater the total influence, the greater the likelihood that a significant, positive correlation will be generated between each minority group and policy expenditure. If our minority groups present positive, significant partial correlations, then we might expect significant, but negative, partial correlations between Republican and Democratic males (other than blacks or Hispanics) and each policy expenditure. This simply presumes that as their influence decreases (and minority group influence increases) in chambers they control, these policies will probably have greater support.

Group influence is operationalized as the sum of representation in 1985 and total influence in 1983, 1985, and 1987. Including 1983 and 1987 data points increases the number of cases, but it fits my perception of the exercise of power. Events, like the support of these policies, are never contemporary or discrete. Influence is a function of the past exercise of power, today's, and the expectations of tomorrow's exercise of power.

Whether all these groups function as expected is uncertain, given their partisan differences. I am particularly uncertain whether positive correlations will be discovered between each of these policy expenditures and Republican Hispanics and other females. For this reason, I intend to pursue this analysis for each group in chambers their party controls and assess whether this influence is effective in unified Democratic state governments, unified Republican state governments, and where there is divided control of government. Where governments are unified, I expect that policy initiatives from the governor will probably reflect less parochial concerns based on legislative districts. If so, there is likely to be an interesting variation in legislative responses. Would a Republican or Democratic unified government strengthen or reverse partial correlations found in chambers controlled by parties. There may be significant differences because governors may have to respond to a larger, more varied constituency for purposes of reelection or a bid for higher office in the coming years.

I use partial correlational analysis in which income will be a controlled variable. Generally, state per capita income is strongly correlated with most policy expenditures. Program funding is a function of the revenues a state can collect, and if per capita income is high, a state can afford to pay more for education, social welfare services, and mental health and hospitals. Of course, there must be a willingness to pursue these goals within the states. I am assuming that this willingness is associated with women, black, and Hispanic influence and their policy preferences. All minority groups are likely, but only likely, to support these expenditures. One must remember that Republicans and Democrats may agree on a number of broad, general goals, but when it comes to spending large sums of money for government (rather than a private sector solution), there may be some differences over the specific means to achieve these goals. This is the essence of policy conflict in U.S. state legislatures.

CONTROL OF CHAMBERS, GOVERNMENTS, AND POLICY INFLUENCE IN THE STATES

The Democrats

Democratic minority groups should ideally support the per capita expenditures for education, social services, and mental health and hospitals. This assessment is due in large part to the perception that they are likely to receive support from constituencies who value these policies: liberals, blacks, and Hispanics. Historically, the Democratic Party has been a supporter of ethnic, racial, and religious minority demands, and these policies are important concerns to each. In fact, this is increasingly likely to occur in southern states where the erosion of white support for the Democratic Party necessitates greater dependence on a coalition that includes black voters. For this reason, it may be foolish to assume that in all cases greater influence among other males will only project negative partial correlations. However uncertain I am, it would seem logical to assume that the partial correlations ought to be negative; I expect positive partial correlations between each minority group's total influence and each of the three policy expenditures.

The results reported in Table 5.8 comprise only those chambers controlled by the Democratic Party (number of cases equals 91), and in only 41 of these cases is there unified Democratic control of government. There are a number of partial correlations that are at variance with my original expectations. This is not true of Democratic males, who manifest negative partial correlation, although the only significant partial correlation is with educational expenditures (−.42, sig. < .000). As male total influence increases, per capita educational expenditures are likely to decline significantly. The minute, insignificant partial correlations with social services (−.01, NS) and mental health and hospitals (−.04, NS)

TABLE 5.8
Partial Correlations between 1985 Per Capita Expenditures for Education, Social Services, and Mental Health/Hospitals and Democratic Groups' Total Potential Influence in Democratically Controlled Chambers and Unified Democratic Governments

Policy Expenditures	Democratic Groups							
	Males*		Females*		Blacks		Hispanics	
Democratic Controlled Chambers (cases = 91)								
Education	−.42	a	.33	a	−.23	c	.39	a
Social Services	−.004	NS	.08	NS	.04	NS	−.09	NS
Mental Health/Hospitals	−.04	NS	−.15	d	.13	d	.05	NS
Unified Democratic Governments (cases = 41)								
Education	−.49	a	.50	a	−.05	NS	.01	NS
Social Services	−.01	NS	.35	b	−.21	d	−.37	b
Mental Health/Hospitals	.02	NS	−.32	c	.42	b	−.18	NS

*Other than blacks and Hispanics.
Significance: a = < .001; b = < .01; c = < .05; d = < .10; NS = not significant.

indicate little male effect, or little interest, in their expenditures. The assumption that males may not have strong interest in these issues is plausible because they are less likely to sponsor human resource legislation.[9]

Among Democratic females (other than blacks and Hispanics), the support for these policies is mixed. Ideally, strong, positive partial correlations with each policy is expected. As female influence increases as a proportion of chamber influence, per capita expenditures for education do increase (.33, sig. < .001), but this is not true for mental health and hospital expenditures (−.15, sig. < .10), indicating the expenditures are greater when women's influence is limited. Again, this is not what an analyst would expect from female Democrats who are likely to be more liberal than their male counterparts.

Perhaps more surprising is the insignificant, but positive correlation, with social service expenditures (.08, NS). The actual expenditure for social services, I think, is the best important indicator of whether groups really support their attendant programs. It appears that the largely white female Democrats do not convert their influence into support for social services. Perhaps, given their small proportion of influence, females represent "closet feminists" who are unwilling to place their careers in jeopardy.[10] This may be even more true during the conservative 1980s where liberal has become the terrible "L" word. After all, women do support education expenditures that can be acceptable to their constituencies. Social service program expenditures are likely to be viewed very stereotypically by white constituents; they favor other constituencies, blacks, and Hispanics, who are linked to the problems of big taxes and profligate expenditures that have not solved the problems of poverty.

One cannot discount, however, that in a time of slow economic growth in most states, there was less willingness to support redistributive programs for other constituencies. These values were enunciated by President Ronald Reagan when he blamed teen pregnancy, family breakups, and worsening poverty on increased welfare dependency. His domestic program cuts had the effect of increasing state and local taxes by an average of 35 percent during this period. It should also be noted that the poor, less-well organized did not have their social service program cuts entirely replaced by the states.[11]

Black partial correlations also represent some unexpected results. Surprisingly, there is a significant, but negative partial correlation (−.23, sig. < .05), with education, a small positive, but insignificant relationship (.04, NS), with social services, and a marginally positive relationship (.13, sig. < .10) with mental health and hospitals. These findings indicate educational expenditures are likely to be lower if black influence is greater. This is difficult to fully understand, unless economic stagnation has temporarily increased the importance of more immediate needs in health care and, certainly, social services. Mental health and hospital expenditures are marginally greater as black influence increases, but one would expect social service expenditures to rise in states with influential black Democrats. This has not occurred, and perhaps it is due to the difficult situation facing the states in the 1980s. Economic stagnation and the need to reduce budget deficits, coupled with poorly organized constituencies that do not exhibit strong participatory behavior, have neutralized the effect of black influence on important social service programs.

Hispanic influence on these policy expenditures are also mixed. The greater the influence of Hispanics, the greater the per capita expenditures for education. The Hispanic community is generally concerned about education, certainly in a symbolic sense associated with Hispanic culture and in terms of developing the skills necessary for social mobility. Although this fits my initial assumptions, the small, insignificant negative correlation with social services expenditures (−.09, NS) is intriguing.

Again, we might suggest that stagnant economies in the eight states with large Hispanic populations preclude a more positive effect. The minute, positive correlation (0.5, NS) with mental health and hospitals may also represent the economic problems facing each of the states with large Hispanic populations.

The state involvement in mental health and hospital expenditures may also suggest problems with mental health establishments concerned about that public involvement. The provision of program dollars by the states may also suggest further efforts to manage or regulate health policy. Because the medical establishment can provide significant funds in political campaigns, it may be important to assess the effects of unified Democratic government on minority relationships with these policy expenditures. In doing so, I submit that the initiatives of a Democratic governor are likely to be sensitive to groups that could affect control of the governor's mansion, even of state house seats.

The total influence of Democratic groups and the correlation with these three program expenditures are somewhat different when there is unified government. Table 5.8 (second section, which represents 41 cases) indicates that the partial correlations of Democratic males with these expenditures do not appreciably change. A strong, negative partial correlation with educational expenditures (−.49, sig. < .000) remains much the same. These expenditures are greater in states as male influence declines. It is difficult to believe that males are likely to be draconian when facing education expenditures. Perhaps, there are cultural factors in these states that provoke limitations in educational expenditures regardless of male or minority influence. Male influence has no significant impact on social services (−.01, NS) or mental health and hospital expenditures (.02, NS). Again, it would appear that there may be little interest in these policy objectives, and their influence has no impact on the level of expenditures.

The impact of a unified government environment is quite dramatic for Democratic women, blacks, and Hispanics. Democratic women's influence is more strongly related to increased educational expenditures in these states (.50, sig. < .000). As women's influence increases, expenditures sharply increase for education. The same is true for social services expenditures. In chambers where I merely took into account whether chambers were controlled by Democrats, women's influence has no real significant impact on social services. In states with unified Democratic control of government, a strong, positive partial correlation (.35, sig. < .01) exists between female influence and social service expenditures. When female influence increases, levels of social service expenditures also increase. This is in keeping with values associated with the nurturing female politician.

However, there is a sharp, significant, and negative correlation between their influence and mental health and hospital expenditures. This is contrary to my expectations and, in fact, may be due to the influence of medical interest groups who are likely to be more active in opposition if groups commonly believed to be liberal increase their influence. This is only a guess. Perhaps this opposition has a negative effect on gubernatorial policy directed at this policy arena. One must remember that this is one area of crisis management that governors are not likely to control very well. In any case, as expected, the larger programs associated with education and social services seem to reflect important support made by Democratic females.

Black influence in states with a unified Democratic government produces different results than reported above. The only policy expenditure that is significantly and positively correlated with black influence is mental health and hospitals. It is significantly stronger (.42, sig. < .01), indicating that the expenditures increase as black influence in state legislatures increases. This is in keeping with what might be expected of black influence, but the partial correlation with social services is unexpected. The results reported above indicated a positive, but insignificant, relationship between black influence and social service expenditures. That relationship is reversed here. I have found that there is marginally significant, but negative, correlation between black influence and social service expenditures (−.21, sig. < .10). If black influence increases from state to state, per capita expenditures for social services tend to decline.

I can only wonder if this is due to serious economic problems and a struggle over increases in taxes to fund programs recently cut by the national government. One may infer that blacks have lost this conflict and that their social service program expenditures are not keeping pace with the negative effects of the Reagan domestic policy cuts or the stagnant economy. Then, too, not many states take responsibility for urban problems, and it is unpopular to be a liberal, that is, give money to nonworking minorities and, therefore, raise state taxes.

The relationship with education expenditures has also changed. Research findings reported in Table 5.8 indicate a significant, negative partial correlation between black influence and education expenditures. This relationship does not exist in states dominated by unified Democratic government. Although no significant relationship exists between black influence and education expenditures, it is a better situation (−.05, NS).

One cannot posit opposition within these governments to the likely effect of black influence. Of course, it is clear that black influence is not significant in this policy arena, but it does raise some interesting questions about where the program dollars may go. Generally white female influence is positively correlated with educational expenditures. Do Democratic females support education where the program dollars are needed, or do they support the expenditures because they are directed toward their white constituencies (if such a conflict exists within a state)? This research has not addressed this question, but I think it is clearly important if we are to label the support for education as a liberal position. The question is particularly important when one considers that many states have serious economic and associated budgetary problems in the 1980s.

Hispanic influence is also different in these Democratic states. Previous findings indicated a significant positive relationship between their influence and educational expenditures and an insignificant, negative relationship with social service expenditures. In these states, their influence is not significantly correlated with education expenditures (.01, NS), but it is negatively and marginally significant when correlated with social service expenditures. As Hispanic influence increases, social services expenditures tend to decline, but there is no real effect on educational expenditures. Their influence is also more negatively correlated with mental health and hospital expenditures.

In summary, it would appear that our expectations about the effect of minority influence are not fulfilled in this analysis. Certainly, Democratic females seem to project the appropriate positive correlations with education and social service expenditures but not with mental health and hospital expenditures. Black influence has positive effects on mental health and hospital expenditures, but the lack of a significant relationship with education, and a negative correlation with social service expenditures, indicates their influence is not translated into policies likely to have a positive effect on their impoverished constituencies. Other political actors are more important. Similar assumptions can be made about Hispanic influence. Either there is no sense of influence where educational expenditures are concerned, or there is an inverse relationship between their influence and social services and mental health and hospital expenditures. Clearly, their influence is not projected as I would expect. I can no longer assert that Democratic gubernatorial initiatives may reflect support for policies associated with minority interests, especially black and Hispanic interests. One may argue this is at least largely true in assessing the effect of female influence.

The Republicans

The partial correlations reported in Table 5.9 illustrate the importance of differentiating these minority groups by party membership. The correlations of Republican groups' total influence with the policy expenditures in chambers they control have a number of surprises. Unfortunately, there are only 36 cases where Republicans control chambers; therefore, some caution is needed in the interpretation. There are also only 12 instances of state governments under unified Republicans. This further limits our analysis. However, it should be noted that each condition represents the universe of Republican control during the time frame of this research.

Unlike Democratic males, Republican males' influence is marginally, but positively, correlated with educational per capita expenditures (.23, sig. < .10). In these chambers, then, the increase in male influence means that per capita expenditures are likely to increase. The same is not true of Republican females. When their influence tends to decline, educational expenditures tend to rise (–.25, sig. < .10). This represents a marginal partial correlation. Democratic females' total influence has a very different effect in Democratically controlled chambers; it is significantly positive.

TABLE 5.9
Partial Correlations between 1985 Per Capita Expenditures for Education, Social Services, and Mental Health/Hospitals and Republican Groups' Total Potential Influence in Republican Controlled Chambers and Unified Republican Governments

| Policy Expenditures | Republican Groups | | |
	Males*	Females*	Hispanics
Republican Controlled Chambers (cases = 36)			
Education	.29 d	–.25 d	.16 NS
Social Services	–.13 NS	.09 NS	.10 NS
Mental Health/Hospitals	.001 NS	.002 NS	–.17 NS
Unified Republican Governments (cases = 12)			
Education	.51 c	–.52 c	.38 d
Social Services	.13 NS	–.12 NS	–.59 b
Mental Health/Hospitals	.41 d	–.40 d	–.06 NS

*Other than Hispanics.
Significance: b = < .01; c = < .05; d = < .10; NS = not significant.

These findings raise serious questions about analyses that simply assess the effects of all women on policy outcomes. Weighing partisan differences is imperative.

Partial correlations between Republican male influence and social service expenditures are negative, although not significant (−.13, NS). If one assesses the effect of Democratic males (and females) in chambers they control, Republican male influence is the only correlation that suggests an inverse relationship between their influence and these expenditures. This is what one would expect in the literature; however, one would also expect Republican females to have a positive relationship with the same expenditures. These expectations are not met; in fact, only a minute, positive correlation between female total influence and social service expenditures is found (.09, NS). Given its size, it would be analytically unwise to actually suggest that as female influence increases, per capita expenditures for social services are also likely to increase. Comparisons with Democratic females in the same circumstances are very difficult because absolutely insignificant relationships are found between their influence and social service expenditures.

Republican males' and females' correlations with mental health and hospital expenditures indicate that their influence has no effect. Both partial correlations are near zero (.001 for males and .002 for females) and are quite similar to the effects of Democratic male influence in their controlled chambers. Of these generally white political groups, only Democratic female influence has a marginal, inverse relationship with these expenditures. Again, these findings are not expected and surprise this author.

Among Republican Hispanics, there is an insignificant, positive correlation with education expenditures (.16, NS), a positive relationship shared with their Hispanic peers across the aisle. Beyond that relationship, there are at best muddled differences over social service and mental health and hospital per capita expenditures. Republican Hispanic influence has an insignificant correlation with social service expenditures (.06, NS) and a negative, but insignificant, relationship with mental health and hospital per capita expenditures (−.17, NS), suggesting it would be inappropriate to assume all Hispanic influence ought to translate into greater expenditures. Among Democratic Hispanics in chambers controlled by Democrats, there was no significant relationship between their influence and these latter two policy expenditures.

There are only 12 cases of unified Republican governments, but the effect of assessing group influence in these chambers is exceptionally dramatic. One would not expect to find any significant partial correlations, but there are six significant and marginally significant relationships. Again, the effect of partisan differences is crucial in these analyses.

Policy expenditures for education, social services, and mental health and hospitals, surprisingly, are positively correlated with Republican male influence. In the environment of unified Republican governments, their increasing influence translates into greater expenditures. Positive, significant correlations exist between their influence and educational expenditures (.51, sig. < .05). There is an insignificant positive correlation with social service expenditures (.13, NS), but it at least suggests a positive relationship with these program expenditures. Finally, there is a marginally significant, but positive, correlation with mental health and hospital policy outcomes (.41, sig. < .10). In fact, one might suggest that their influence performs much like Democratic female influence with the exception of mental health and hospital policy expenditures (inverse relationship exists for Democratic females). Their influence also functions very differently from black Democratic influence in unified Democratic chambers, with the exception of mental health and hospital expenditures. These findings are surprising and raise questions about the definitions of liberal and conservative.

Does this mean males are the liberals of the Republican Party? If positive correlations are the definition of liberal, then they are, and Republican females are conservatives. Republican females have inverse relationships with each of these policy expenditures.

Female influence has a significant, inverse relationship with educational expenditures (−.52, sig. < .05) in states under unified Republican control. This is surprising given expectation of female policy interest, even more startling because this relationship is at variance with the effects of male influence. The partial correlation with social service expenditures is insignificant (−.12, NS), but I think one can assume an inverse tendency exists. Finally, there is also an inverse, marginally significant, correlation with mental health and hospital expenditures (−.40, sig. < .10).

It may be easy to explain female correlations as the effect of difficult economic times in the states Republicans govern. However, the male relationship with each of these expenditures, clearly in a different direction, makes this assumption at best difficult. Apparently, and this is very obvious, male influence, quite dominant in each of these states, sets policy direction. Does this overwhelming male dominance in influence create an extreme "closet feminist" reaction among Republican females as a group, or does this represent a rationalization? Is it possible that a self-selection process is at work? Perhaps, through self-selection, the successful female candidates for Republican seats may tend to be more conservative, perhaps more "extreme" ideologically, than their male counterparts. They are quite different from Democratic females. Generally, Democratic females as a group project a positive relationship with program outcomes (the exception is mental health). Or is there a real difference in how power is manipulated in unified Democratic and Republican states that could affect this gender difference? Ascertaining whether this is true is not possible with this study. I think it may become essential to change the level of analysis from state differences to leadership behavior within each party and then compare them.

It is interesting to note that Republican Hispanics' influence is functioning differently on each expenditure. Hispanic influence has a positive, marginal relationship with educational expenditures (.38, sig. < .10) and a strong negative correlation with social services (−.59, sig. < .01). Each of these correlations makes sense. One would expect strong support for education policy in this minority group. The inverse relationship between social service expenditures and Hispanic influence is due, I think, to the large proportion of active middle-class Cuban-Americans in this study. The Hispanic Republican relationship to social services is stronger, but the direction is similar to that of Hispanic Democrats. There is no significant relationship with mental health and hospital expenditures (−.06, NS), which could suggest a direction, although Democratic Hispanics do have a negative correlation with the same policy. Even then, it is difficult to affirm strong similarities between these different ethnic Republican and Democratic groups.

Incorporation of Republican and Democratic groups in the state legislatures varies a great deal. Influence, due in large part to greater representation, rests with Democratic and Republican males. Within the Democratic Party, women's influence has slightly increased whereas black influence is quite variable, declining in party leadership positions and remaining stable when one includes committee chairs as an index of their influence. Hispanic influence is relatively stable during these years. Republican Party influence is largely male influence, and, in fact, female influence overall has declined very slightly. Hispanic influence within the Republican Party is negligible at best, primarily due to the minority status of their party.

The assumption that representation should predict the incorporation of minority groups in leadership positions is also variable. It is variable depending if you are referring to party leadership positions or total influence, which incorporates party leadership and committee chairs as a single index. The prediction of black party leadership declines during each passing election, but, by including committee chairs (total influence), a large percentage of variance (between 50 percent and 60 percent) is explained. The proportion of variance explained by representation for Hispanic Democrats is even higher, perhaps due to the skewedness of the data. Nevertheless, it is extremely significant as a response to their future influence. Female influence in the Democratic Party is erratically predicted indicating that personality, chamber traditions, or state cultural values may play a role in the influence obtained in state legislatures.

Republican group influence is not strongly predicted in 1983, but it does increase to significant levels following each succeeding election to above 40 percent of the variance explained. Republican Hispanic representation does not predict their influence in chambers.

Perhaps the most important factor associated with incorporation (representation plus total chamber influence) is whether it predicts policy per capita expenditures in education, social services, and mental health and hospitals. The choice of three human resource per capita expenditures was based on existing perceptions in the literature that assumed each of these minorities was positively interested in these policy outcomes. If each group was supportive, one could only assume that as their influence grew in chambers, that influence would significantly and positively predict policy outcomes. There were surprises that necessitate a partisan differentiation of minority groups. It is obvious that Democratic female influence (in unified Democratic states) translates into increased expenditures in educational and social service programs. This is as predicted. But, Republican female influence represents inverse relationships in Republican unified states. Apparently, research can no longer analyze women as a single group moving in a liberal direction.

The same seems to be true of blacks and Hispanics. The direction of partial correlations with different policy expenditures tends to vary and raises important questions about the use of power in chambers and its relationship to constituents. Can one suggest that this correlation may reflect intense political conflict between whites and blacks? The assessment of variables predicting black representation may indicate this is the case. The declining ability of representation to predict more visible leadership roles in the Democratic Party must also give pause to serious reflection. Being liberal has become, stereotypically, an unpopular position because it is assumed that poor, nonworking minorities are receiving support that is sharply increasing taxes. One should also remember that very few states take a positive role in dealing with urban problems. In fact, state governments often seem to be antagonistic, and this would certainly affect these human resource programs regardless of black influence.

The relationship between influence and gender in the Republican Party, particularly in unified Republican states, is startling. The inverse relationships between female influence and the three policies raise serious questions. When their influence increases, per capita expenditures tend to marginally, significantly, or slightly decline. This is obviously not in keeping with assumptions of women's influence and how it might be used. Clearly partisan differences matter here. It would appear that although ambiguous, positive goals associated with a symbolic position on, for example, the Equal Rights Amendment are considered, no difference is likely between Democratic and Republican females. But, ideologically, what role is government to perform? Is its role to be expanded or decreased, because the private sector can achieve these goals more economically and efficiently? Or, does this research simply project the ambiguities often found in correlational research that uses state characteristics to describe and predict political action or influence?

Given the clear positive and negative correlations associated with gender in the Democratic and especially the Republican parties, I think partisan, ideological differences are at work. Perhaps Republican females, to win elections, to obtain influence, tend to be more extreme in terms of their conservative values, even more extreme than their Republican peers in unified Republican states.

Although I have no evidence for this, the level of analysis is inappropriate, I reflect on two Republican challengers to the General Assembly in my midwestern area. The woman was very conservative, especially on the issue of abortion, which was impermissible even in cases of rape or incest. The male was pro-choice. Both lost the election, but it was the extreme position on abortion that defeated the woman.

The differences between Democratic and Republican Hispanics can be explained by ethnic and class distinctions. Cuban-American influence is inversely related to social service expenditures, and this is also true of Democratic Hispanics. The reason for the inverse relationship with Democratic influence can be found in the explanation of black influence. States do not strongly support policies to solve urban problems. Economic problems in the 1980s abound, and it just is not popular to support increased expenditures to nonworking minorities and ask for tax increases to do so. That popular perception is held by many Americans, and they happen to represent a majority of voters.

The importance of partisan distinctions becomes clearer in the assessment of group influence and the effect on policy outcomes. Much about influence in chambers remains unexplained. Incorporation in terms of influence is quite obviously related to the representation obtained in legislative chambers, particularly in the dominant political parties.

NOTES

1. See the three publications by the Council of State Governments, *State Legislative Leadership, Committees, and Staff, 1983–84, 1985–86, 1987–88* (Lexington: Council of State Governments, 1983, 1985, 1987).

2. Albert J. Nelson, "Women's Potential Influence in Lower State Legislative Chambers," *Wisconsin Political Scientist* 2 (Fall 1987): 5–13.

3. See Charles Lindbloom, *Politics and Markets* (New York: Basic Books, 1977); Mancur Olson, *The Rise and Decline of Nations* (New Haven: Yale University Press, 1982).

4. Alan Rosenthal, *Legislative Life* (New York: Harper & Row, 1981).

5. These are reported in the Council of State Governments' publications noted in note 1 above. One should be aware that minority leadership positions might be underreported and that where committee leadership positions are concerned, few ranking members are reported.

6. See Susan Welch, "Are Women More Liberal Than Men in the U.S. Congress?" *Legislative Studies Quarterly* 10 (February 1985): 125–34; Sue Thomas and Susan Welch, "'The Impact of Gender on Activities and Priorities of State Legislators." Paper presented at the Annual 1989 Meeting of the Midwest Political Science Association, Chicago, Illinois; Sue Thomas, "The Impact of Women on State Legislative Policies." Paper presented at the 1989 Annual Meeting of the American Political Science Association, Atlanta, Georgia.

7. Rosenthal, *Legislative Life.*

8. Irene Diamond, *Sex Roles in the State House* (New Haven: Yale University Press, 1977); Janet A. Flammang, "Female Officials in the Feminist Capital: The Case of Santa Clara County," *Western Political Quarterly* 38 (March 1985): 94–118; Welch, "Are Women More Liberal?"

9. Margery M. Ambrosius and Susan Welch, "State Legislators' Perceptions of Business and Labor Interests," *Legislative Studies Quarterly* 13 (May 1988): 199–209; Robert Y. Shapiro and Mahajan Harprett, "Gender Differences in Policy Preferences: A Summary of Trends from the 1960s to the 1980s," *Public Opinion Quarterly* 50 (1986): 42–61.

10. Susan J. Carroll, "Women Candidates and Support for Feminist Concerns: The Closet Feminist Syndrome," *Western Political Quarterly* 37 (June 1984): 307–23.

11. B. B. Kymlicka and Jean V. Matthews, eds., *The Reagan Revolution?* (Chicago: Dorsey Press, 1980); *New York Times,* February 16, 1986, p. 27a.

6

SUMMARIZING
INCORPORATION DYNAMICS

My approach to minority incorporation includes research strategies that help clarify the explanations of representation, turnover, and influence on policy expenditures. Assessing the influence of minority groups must be concerned with several factors. First, it is obvious that they must obtain representation within legislative chambers to have any effect at all. Most research does address this, and it is the simplest assumption to make. Perhaps more important, an analysis of representation would be better served if it differentiated the minority groups by their partisan attachments. One must be aware that Roman Catholic ethnic voters are traditional constituents of Democrats in the North and that conservative Protestants are traditional grassroots voters in the South.

There is another aspect associated with partisanship. How influential is a group? Much of the research now assumes that each minority must be dealt with as a single group. In large part, this thinking is tied to the assumption that each group is an important, symbolic role model to the larger community. Minorities must be viewed to be more than symbolic role models to the groups they represent. Although being political role models is still important, each group is much more important than that.

Women, blacks and Hispanics must be viewed for who they are as politicians. They have partisan preferences and often face tough choices that are affected by their value preferences. This may be less of an analytical problem when dealing with blacks who are Democrats, but it becomes a serious problem when we are concerned about females and Hispanics who are either Republicans or Democrats. For example, simply assuming that women's 18 percent in a Democratic chamber is an indicator of influence neglects the simple fact that a large portion of that figure represents Republican women. Further, the Republican Party controls only a small portion of the chambers in this study, and the Democratic Party controls twice as many. One should also direct this assessment at Hispanics.

Representation in this sense is quite relative. Do minority members belong to the majority party where they have an opportunity to control the policy agenda as party leaders and committee chairpersons? Only then can one seriously assess their effect on policy outcomes. Certainly the partial correlations between group influence and policy expenditures in Chapter 5 render this approach to be entirely valid.

Second, one must address minority representation within parties. Power, as noted above, is obtained from membership in a legislature's majority party. I thought that this would give us a different perspective about representation. In fact, representation within political parties was not that different from the analysis of partisan minority representation in chambers. However, it did allow me to compare gender differences. This research strategy has allowed me to do more than simply pose questions about blacks, Hispanics, or women's influence. In Chapter 3, I began to address important comparisons with the two dominant groups in state legislatures: other (than blacks and Hispanics) Republican and Democratic males. The comparison of, for example, Democratic male and female representation within political parties is very important in clearly explaining why Democratic women took more time to achieve parity with their Republican peers. It also tells us more about the dynamics of politics between the genders. When an inverse relationship exists between traditional supporters of the Democratic Party (Roman Catholics and conservative Protestants) and Democratic female representation, and positive relationships exist with Democratic males, it is also quite clear why women have not had an opportunity to achieve parity with males. Similar factors exist within the Republican Party as well.

I also think it very important to recognize that this conservative era's major issues can be explained by religious beliefs. Religion has an impact on occupational choices, and the choices may also affect political opportunity. How traditional Roman Catholics and conservative Protestants assess female politicians will probably affect their political mobility. I know women's influence has been relatively stagnant during each of these three elections. But in spite of religious opposition, which is assumed in a conservative era where abortion is very important, Democratic women were able to achieve parity with Republican women. That is no small accomplishment when one also considers that local party organizations were not very helpful in obtaining political office.

Finally, it is important to pursue a longitudinal analysis of representation, turnover, and influence in state legislatures. I had hoped that either the presidential election in 1984, the apportionment/economic recession, or the off-year, Iran-Contra election would have a significant impact on representation. None of them had this effect on representation, but the presidential election did significantly decrease Republican turnover in 1984. Perhaps more important, it did allow me a large pool of data points to assess representation in the North and South. This has enhanced my understanding of the effects each region has on minority groups, particularly black representatives.

WOMEN IN STATE LEGISLATURES

The Democrats

A general discussion of each minority group begins with partisan differences, an important aspect of incorporation. For example, Democratic women, simply by the number of chambers their party controls, and the number of unified Democratic governments, have far greater influence than their Republican sisters. Their representation is likely to occur in states with metropolitan characteristics and where a larger proportion of women are employed. This is an important characteristic because it assumes that as women enter the economy outside the home, their political interest, efficacy, and participation will increase. As it does, more women run for office and win. This independent variable remains an important factor explaining representation among Democratic women although their representation does not appreciably increase in chambers or within their party during this period.

Democratic women have achieved parity with Republican females and, therefore, have more political clout because their party controls many more chambers. I believe the reasons their representation lagged have much to do with the conservative era and their grassroots constituency. The triumph of conservative politics represents in part a conflict over social services to nonworking minorities, high taxes, and abortion. Democrats, and therefore female Democrats, are stereotyped as liberals, a terrible nuance likely to be associated with feminists. Democratic women must seek support among the Roman Catholics of northern metropolitan states and among conservative Protestants (fundamentalists, charismatics, evangelicals) in the South. The latter will not support feminists, and both religious groups will not support candidates who are likely to support abortion. As indicated earlier, religious beliefs structure employment and also structure political opportunities. For these reasons, Democratic women are likely to do well if there are fewer Roman Catholics and conservative Protestants in their constituencies.

Their predicament is made more difficult when one recognizes that they do better if local Democratic organizations are weak and less capable of blocking their political ambitions. When one compares these religious and party organizational effects on Democratic males, opposite relationships between religion or no impact by Democratic organizations are found. Religion mixes with politics and represents serious barriers to Democratic women as politicians. Even a local Democratic party organization represents a marginally significant barrier to their success.

Democratic females' turnover is quite similar to their male peers' turnover as a percentage of their own representation and greater as a percentage of their representation than blacks. When one compares real turnover, male turnover is actually five and six to one greater than female turnover. This ratio is even greater in the South. In terms of total turnover, it means that more seats are open where there once were male incumbents. Still, women's representation remains stable following each election. There is an assumption that incumbency is a major factor that stymies their representation, but this must implicitly assume that females remain in office. For whatever reasons, female Democrats leave these legislative offices as often as their male peers. Nor do they gain many of the seats left vacant by their male colleagues. Other factors must also come into play, and I would think they have much to do with those grassroots supporters crucial to Democratic success.

The parity achieved with Republican women in legislative chambers in the 1980s has slightly increased Democratic women's political influence. Influence has increased in Democratically controlled chambers, but it has not reached parity with women's actual representation in the Democratic Party. Their influence has sharply increased in chambers controlled by Republicans. In reality, this reinforces expectations of women's influence: there will be an inverse relationship between the power of an office and the women in the office. Being a Democratic leader in a Republican controlled chamber represents a symbolic rather than substantive influence. In fact, while women's representation significantly predicts their influence in chambers, a majority of the variance remains unexplained. One must factor in leadership decisions, personality, legislative traditions, and customs, which vary from state to state and affect leadership recruitment.

I assumed from literature reviews that women are likely to sponsor and support human resource issues like education, social service programs, and mental health and hospital per capita expenditures. In states with unified Democratic governments, I expected that as the influence of women increased, per capita expenditures would also increase while controlling for state per capita income. This was the case for education and social services; however, there was a significant, inverse relationship with mental health and hospital expenditures. Among Democratic males, a significant inverse relationship exists between their influence and educational expenditures, but no significant relationships exist with the remaining policy expenditures. In a real sense, one could stipulate that Democratic females are in fact liberal supporters of human resource policies. This should have important consequences in the 1990s based on the events of the 1990 election. I believe that as the dominant issues shift to fairness, Democratic women will benefit. Concern about fair taxes and a number of social issues should enhance their political support and representation and should increase their political influence. I am uncertain if the same could be said for Republican women if the tide of public opinion moves toward Democratic issues.

The Republicans

Republican women were more successful than their Democratic peers in the 1970s, but that success was equaled by 1987 in chambers. However, it should be noted that Republican women represented a larger percentage of the Republican Party. As representatives of a party associated with professional classes, it is no surprise that the most important predictor of their representation is the percent of females employed. They also represent states with metropolitan characteristics (probably suburban areas), and, as I would expect, their success is greater if there are fewer Roman Catholics and conservative Protestants in those states. Politically, these religious groups support Democrats, depending on the region being investigated. As expected, weak Democratic organizations enhance the likelihood of their political success. In these relationships, they seemingly share much with Democratic women, but the reality is that Democratic women face significant barriers to their success within their traditional constituencies in addition to their own party.

If one compares representation within the Republican Party, other factors emerge suggesting religious beliefs and party organizational dynamics have different effects based on gender. The most important factor remains the percent of females employed outside the home, but the inverse relationship between females and conservative Protestants is not shared by males. The Republican Party is making inroads in the South, but that support is more likely directed toward males who have a strong positive relationship with these Protestants. It is also interesting to note that if Democratic organizations are weak, males do very well whereas no significant relationship exists for females.

But two party organizational factors do suggest problems for Republican females. Males are likely to do well in traditional party organization states and where the Republican Party is strongly organized. Republican women do not do well in traditional party organization states, and, although the Republican Party organization is no significant predictor of their representation (an important difference), the direction of that relationship suggests we can assume that a less capable Republican Party is better than one that is effective. Turnover in the Republican Party indicates that it is greater among males following the 1982 election, but it becomes similar for males and females following the 1984 and 1986 elections. Turnover decreases in 1984 because of the party's success in the presidential election, but it increases for females during 1986. Still, the turnover of the 1986 election is less than that which occurred in 1982. Compared to the turnover that occurs among males in the Republican Party, turnover is far less for females. Apparently, females have not been able, like Democratic females, to win these seats because their representation in chambers and in their party remains stable.

The independent variables that predict female turnover are most often due to shifts toward Democratic control of formerly Republican chambers. It also occurs in states where there is a high percentage of employed females, the most important predictor of their representation. The variance explained by the regression analysis of their turnover is less than that which predicts their representation.

Female influence in the Republican party is actually greater than their Democratic peers in their own party following the 1982 and 1984 elections. However, it declines to its lowest point after the 1986 election while Democratic female influence increases in their party. The same is true for their total influence (party leadership and committee chairpersons). It is greater than their Democratic peers following the first two elections, but it falls after the 1986 election below the influence of Democratic females. It is intriguing to note that female representation does not predict their influence in 1983, but it increasingly becomes an important predictor of their influence in 1985 and 1987. I think it is clear that, as with Democratic females, one could assume that leadership preferences, personality, customs, and traditions not assessed by this analysis would probably provide much of the explanation for their influence.

The partisan differences I assume to be important become quite clear in the assessment of influence and its relationship to the human resource policy expenditures. Within unified Republican governments, Republican female influence has a consistent inverse relationship with education, social services, and mental health and hospital expenditures. Although the relationship is not significant with social services, the direction of that relationship is negative. Male Republican influence translates into greater per capita expenditures in each policy arena. This is unlike their female peers because an increase in Republican female influence means per capita expenditures are likely to decline. Who is conservative or at least moderate on the basis of this research focusing on unified Republican governments? Republican males?

Assessing these relationships, I wondered if it were possible that a self-selection process occurs among females in the Republican Party. Are they more conservative than their male peers, or do they represent a more extreme form of closet feminism? Clearly, the partisan differentiation of females has, at the very least, yielded important questions about policy preferences that would not be obtained without differentiating partisanship.

BLACKS AND HISPANICS IN STATE LEGISLATURES

The Black Democrats

In many respects, the analysis of black representation is much like that of their female Democratic peers. When I assess their representation in chambers, it is obvious that they do better in metropolitan states where Democratic organizations are weak or in decline. Nationally, there are negative *betas* associated with Roman Catholic and conservative Protestant populations. The former is not surprising because, traditionally, Roman Catholic ethnics have controlled local Democratic organizations in metropolitan areas. Here, sharp political conflicts exist, and they are depicted in this analysis. The inverse relationship with conservative Protestantism is surprising because black representation is greater in the South. This relationship is reversed in an analysis of black representation in the North and South. In the North, the proportion of the population that is black is now a key predictor of their representation.

The major dynamic thrust of the findings is to once again depict conflict between local Democratic organizations and Roman Catholic populations. Blacks do better in metropolitan states with weak or declining local Democratic organizations and where there are fewer Roman Catholics. Much like women in their party, the states where they are most successful have had antidiscrimination laws for some time, the population has fewer people with 16 or more years of education, and the ratio between legislative salaries and per capita income tends to be smaller. I believe the relationship with legislative salaries indicates crucial ambiguities, but they could only be solved by using districts within states to ascertain their validity.

The factors that predict southern black representation are quite different. Strong local Democratic organizations and traditional party organization states positively predict their representation. Weak local Republican party organizations are important predictors of their success, as is the proportion of conservative Protestants. Many blacks are Protestants and tend to share religious values with, for example, Southern Baptists. Multimember districts and well-educated states also predict greater black representation. The latter relationship ought to exist because tolerance is associated with increased educational attainment (it is reversed in the North). In essence, the expectations of party organization action are what one might expect in a region in which Democratic success is increasingly dependent on black voters.

Generally, turnover among blacks as a percentage of their representation is smaller than in any other group. This turnover is predicted by the proportion of the state population that is black, but it also is likely to occur where there is a larger Hispanic population. Because both populations reside in metropolitan states, I believe this indicates present and future political conflict in a struggle for power. This conflict will intensify as more Hispanics register and participate. Turnover is also greater in states with multimember districts.

Black influence in the Democratic Party decreases each year during this study, and as it does, so does the predictive effect of their representation. If one adds committee chairs to their influence, their representation does explain a large percentage of the variance. Although this relationship exists now, even if influence decreases, the unusual position of Democratic blacks is that they have nowhere to go. They cannot join the Republican Party even if the Democratic Party does not support their policy preferences. It appears that their influence does not translate into expected, strong correlations with human resource policy expenditures. If anything, the conservative era in which we live hampers this influence: opposition to taxes, human resource services, and blacks, generally, during a period of economic contraction among the general, white population hamstrung black political influence in the 1980s when the Reverend Jesse Jackson was running for president.

The Hispanic Democrats

Democratic Hispanics do not represent a very large group in our study, and their numbers affect the quality of the research findings. Hispanic representation, and their influence, is at best minimal due to low voter registration, and many legal Hispanic residents have yet to become naturalized citizens. Their representation is largely explained in chambers by many of the same factors that predict black and female Democratic success. It is intriguing to note that when one compares the effect of Hispanic population on males and females, the Hispanic population strongly predicts male representation in regions. This variable only weakly predicts female Hispanic political success in state legislatures. I think a major reason for this outcome is the small proportion of Hispanics holding legislative office.

Perhaps the most anomalous finding is the inverse relationship of the Roman Catholic population in states and representation. Nothing could be farther from the truth. This is one of the weaknesses associated with state characteristics that may be due to an incorrect count of Hispanics by the Roman Catholic Church.

Turnover among Hispanics as a percent of their representation in chambers is similar to that of other females in the Democratic Party. As expected, it is likely to occur in states with large Hispanic populations, and it will be greater in those states with smaller legislative districts. Again, the small proportion of Hispanics makes this analysis incomplete. As Hispanics increase their participation, a clear picture of other factors affecting their political experience will be obtained.

Their influence is strongly predicted by their representation and may be due to their future importance in the states and, quite possibly, to the skewedness associated with the small number of states with significant Hispanic populations. The effects of their influence on policy expenditures are at best unexpected, given the assumptions of policy interests. First, no significant relationship exists with education and mental health and hospital per capita expenditures. Finally, there is a significant, but inverse relationship between their influence and social services expenditures. This may reflect a reversal of their small political fortune, much like the effects on black influence.

The Hispanic Republicans

The paucity of Democratic Hispanic representation is an even greater problem when one tries to analyze Hispanic Republicans. I cannot stipulate that minute representation is due to low voter interest, particularly among Cuban-Americans. The problem is that few Hispanic ethnic groups identify, at least at this time, with the Republican Party. Still, their national and northern regional representation within chambers is remarkably similar to that of their Democratic peers. The same is not true in the South. The strong inverse relationships among multimember district states, conservative Protestants, and local Democratic organizations are very different. In fact, Democratic Hispanics are doing well when their party organizations are weak or declining, but Republican Hispanics are doing well, especially in Florida, where the local Democratic parties are well organized and effective. They are unlikely to do well in traditional party organization states, but, once again, the small proportion of Republican Hispanics who reside in Florida skew the findings of this research. Again, caution is a watchword.

The differences between genders within the Republican Party are remarkable for their similarity with Hispanic Democrats. A Hispanic population more strongly predicts male representation and only marginally predicts female representation. Again, there is a problem with numbers because there are very few female Hispanics. Cultural values associated with what is an appropriate male or female role may be extremely effective as they are when we assess other males and females.

In fact, the small numbers of Republican Hispanics mean that turnover is only significantly predicted by the existence of Hispanic communities — not very informative, I daresay. This also extends to the amount of influence they hold in chambers controlled by the Republican Party. The amount is so minuscule that their representation cannot predict it. With this caveat, the correlations existing with policy expenditures are at best uncertain. Education and social services per capita expenditures individually depict a marginal, positive or significant inverse relationship (respectively). No significant relationship exists between their total influence and mental health and hospital per capita expenditures. I believe each of these findings associated with Republican Hispanics must have a cautionary note attached. Each finding may be due more to skewedness and, hence, represent an accidental relationship.

FUTURE DIRECTIONS FOR RESEARCH

A number of ambiguities in this research could be addressed if it were to address a different level of analysis. For example, other Democratic and Republican females represent metropolitan states, as do blacks and Hispanics. They all live in metropolitan areas, but we must assume that the essentially white females represent suburban areas of these states. In the North, blacks and Hispanics are likely to be found in central cities. By creating a data base that addresses representation in state assembly districts, or some other viable substitute, I think one can better explain representation, turnover, and why certain positions of influence, for example, in a committee system, are obtained. By changing the level of analysis, one increases the number of cases and the certainty analysts can project in their research efforts. If this is done, greater clarity and far less ambiguity is likely to occur in correlation research.

In order to assess the few Hispanics, especially in the Republican Party, it would probably be necessary to focus the research on the individual. Surveys and in-depth interviews would probably ascertain the factors affecting their recruitment to legislative office, the reasons they leave office, and the intricacies of maneuver and negotiation involved in obtaining party leadership and committee chairs.

Although these are some suggestions to strengthen research, this research has addressed representation, turnover, and influence in a unique fashion. Much of this is possible by pursuing a longitudinal analysis, differentiating partisan membership, and particularly assessing representation within parties. This allows one to address gender differences that would be impossible if one assessed them in chambers. If anything, the gender comparisons offer very real insight into how each is treated very differently within their party. It certainly addressed the lagging representation of Democratic women, particularly by using religious independent variables to assess the effect of traditional constituents in the Democratic Party. The most important rationale for doing so is associated with the source of power formally obtained in legislatures. It is through party membership, and I have not seen much research that has developed this approach.

The research strategies I have used raise interesting questions about the differences between Democratic and Republican females. Obviously, they are not the same, certainly in terms of the correlations found between their influence and support for human resource policy expenditures. Assumptions that they are the same are associated with perceptions of their most important role, a symbolic role model for other women.

Women have moved beyond this role and are pursuing personal and constituent political interests that are often at odds with the liberal orientations of academics. They must function in terms of their own values, driven by events and political calculations to shape their own lives. This is probably true of all the minority groups in this study.

BIBLIOGRAPHY

BOOKS

Addams, Jane. *Twenty Years at Hull House*. New York: New American Library, 1961 (1910).

Axinn, June, and Herman Levine. *Social Welfare: A History of the American Response to Need*. New York: Harper & Row, 1982.

Boswell, Thomas D., and James R. Curtis. *The Cuban-American Experience: Culture, Images, and Perspectives*. Totowa, NJ: Rowman and Allanheld, 1984.

Browning, Rufus P., Dale Roger Marshall, and David H. Tabb. *Protest Is Not Enough: The Struggle of Blacks and Hispanics for Equality in Urban Politics*. Berkeley: University of California, 1984.

Carroll, Susan J. *Women as Candidates in American Politics*. Bloomington: Indiana University Press, 1985.

Cole, Leonard A. *Blacks in Power: A Comparative Study of Black and White Elected Officials*. Princeton: Princeton University Press, 1976.

Council of State Governments. *State Elective Officials and Legislatures, 1983–1984*. Lexington: Council of State Governments, 1983.

____. *State Elective Officials and Legislatures, 1985–1986*. Lexington: Council of State Governments, 1985.

____. *State Elective Officials and Legislatures, 1987–1988*. Lexington: Council of State Governments, 1987.

____. *State Legislative Leadership, Committees, and Staff, 1983–1984*. Lexington: Council of State Governments, 1983.

____. *State Legislative Leadership, Committees, and Staff, 1985–1986*. Lexington: Council of State Governments, 1985.

____. *State Legislative Leadership, Committees, and Staff, 1987–1988*. Lexington: Council of State Governments, 1987.

Dahl, Robert A. *After the Revolution?* New Haven: Yale University Press, 1970.

Darcy, R., Susan Welch, and Janet Clark. *Women, Elections, and Representation*. New York: Longman, 1987.

De la Garza, Rodolfo O., et al., eds. *The Mexican-American Experience: An Interdisciplinary Approach.* Austin: University of Texas Press, 1985.

Diamond, Irene. *Sex Roles in the State House.* New Haven: Yale University Press, 1977.

Elazar, Daniel J. *American Federalism: A View from the States.* New York: Thomas Y. Crowell, 1972.

Fenno, Richard. *Congressmen in Committees.* Boston: Little, Brown, 1973.

Flannigan, William H., and Nancy H. Zingale. *Political Behavior and the American Electorate.* Boston: Allyn and Bacon, 1987.

Ford Foundation. *Hispanics: Challenges and Opportunities.* New York: Ford Foundation, 1984.

Garcia, F. Chris, and Rodolfo O. De la Garza. *The Chicano Experience: Three Perspectives.* North Scituate: Duxbury Press, 1977.

Gastil, Raymond D. *Cultural Regions of the United States.* Seattle: University of Washington Press, 1975.

Grabler, Leo, Joan W. Moore, and Ralph C. Guzman. *The Mexican-American People: The Nation's Second Largest Minority.* New York: Free Press, 1970.

Harris, Fred R. *American Democracy.* Glenview: Scott, Foresman, 1986.

Heilbrun, James. *Urban Economics and Public Policy.* New York: St. Martin's Press, 1982.

Jacob, Herbert, and Kenneth N. Vines, eds. *Politics in the American States.* Boston: Little, Brown, 1965.

Jennings, James, and Monte Rivera, Jr., eds. *Puerto Rican Politics in Urban America.* Westport: Greenwood Press, 1977.

Joint Center for Political Studies (JCPS). *Directory of Black Leadership, 1985.* Washington, D.C.: Joint Center for Political Studies, 1985.

_____. *Directory of Black Leadership, 1987.* Washington, D.C.: JCPS, 1987.

Judd, Dennis R. *The Politics of American Cities.* Boston: Little, Brown, 1988.

Kingdon, John. *Congressmen's Voting Decisions.* New York: Harper & Row, 1982.

Kirkpatrick, Jeanne. *Political Woman.* New York: Basic Books, 1977.

Kymlicka, B. B., and Jean V. Matthews, eds. *The Reagan Revolution?* Chicago: Dorsey Press, 1988.

Lewis-Beck, Michael S. *Applied Regression: An Introduction.* Beverly Hills: Sage, 1980.

Lindbloom, Charles. *Politics and Markets.* New York: Basic Books, 1977.

Lubove, Roy. *The Professional Altruist: The Emergence of Social Work as a Career, 1880–1930.* Cambridge: Harvard University Press, 1965.

Matney, William C. *America's Black Population 1970 to 1982: A Statistical View.* Washington, D.C.: U.S. Government Printing Office, 1983.

Mayhew, David R. *Congress: The Electoral Connection.* New Haven: Yale University Press, 1974.

Nie, Norman H., et al. *SPSSx.* New York: McGraw-Hill, 1986.

Olson, Mancur. *The Rise and Decline of Nations.* New Haven: Yale University Press, 1982.

Pateman, Carole. *Participation and Democratic Theory.* Cambridge: Cambridge University Press, 1970.

Phillips, Kevin. *Post-Conservative America.* New York: Random House, 1982.

Pitkin, Hannah. *The Concept of Representation.* Berkeley: University of California Press, 1967.

Quinn, Bernard, et al. *Churches and Membership in the U.S., 1980.* Atlanta: Glenmary Research Center, 1982.

Rosenthal, Alan. *Legislative Life.* New York: Harper & Row, 1981.

Sapiro, Virginia. *The Political Integration of Women.* Urbana: University of Illinois Press, 1983.

Schlesinger, Joseph. *Ambition and Politics: Political Careers in the United States.* Chicago: Rand, McNally, 1966.

Shepsle, Kenneth A. *The Giant Jigsaw: Democratic Committee Assignments in the Modern House.* Chicago: University of Chicago Press, 1978.

Stark, Rodney, and Charles Y. Glock. *American Piety: The Nature of Religious Commitment.* Berkeley: University of California Press, 1968.

Stroup, Herbert. *Social Welfare Pioneers.* Chicago: Nelson-Hall, 1986.

Trattner, Walter J. *From Poor Law to Welfare State.* New York: Free Press, 1979.

Tufte, Edward R. *The Quantitative Analysis of Social Problems.* Reading; Addison-Wesley, 1970.

U.S. Bureau of Census. *County and City Data Book.* Washington, D.C.: U.S. Government Printing Office, 1983.

____. *Statistical Abstract of the United States.* Washington, D.C.: U.S. Government Printing Office, 1989.

PERIODICALS AND NEWSPAPERS/MAGAZINES

Ambrosius, Margery M., and Susan Welch. "State Legislators' Perceptions of Business and Labor Interests," *Legislative Studies Quarterly* 13 (May 1988): 199–209.

Anderson, Kristi. "Working Women and Political Participation, 1952–1972," *American Journal of Political Science* 19 (August 1975): 439–53.

Bibby, John F. "Patterns of Gubernatorial and State Legislative Elections," *Public Opinion Quarterly* 6 (1983): 41–46.

Bullock III, Charles S. "Congressional Voting and Mobilization of a Black Electorate in the South," *Journal of Politics* 43 (1981): 662–82.

Carroll, Susan J. "Women Candidates and Support for Feminist Concerns: The Closet Feminist Syndrome," *Western Political Quarterly* 37 (June 1984): 307–23.

Campbell, James E. "Presidential Coattails and Midterm Losses in State Legislative Elections," *American Political Science Review* 80 (March 1986): 45–64.

Christian Science Monitor. May 1, 1984, p. 19.

Dubeck, Paula. "Women and Access to Political Office," *The Sociological Quarterly* 17 (1976): 42–52.

Dye, Thomas R. "State Legislative Politics." In Herbert Jacob and Kenneth N. Vines, eds., *Politics in the American States.* Boston: Little, Brown, 1965.

Erickson, Robert S., et al. "Knowing One's District: How Legislators Predict Referendum Voting," *American Journal of Political Science* 19 (1975): 231–46.

Fallows, James. "Immigration: How It's Affecting Us," *The Atlantic Monthly,* November 1983, pp. 45–106.

Flammang, Janet A. "Female Officials in the Feminist Capital: The Case of Santa Clara County," *Western Political Quarterly* 38 (March 1985): 94–118.

Francis, Wayne L., and James Riddlesperger, "U.S. State Legislative Committee Systems: Structure, Procedural Efficiency and Party Control," *Legislative Studies Quarterly* 7 (November 1982): 453–71.

Gibson, James L., et al. "Whither the Local Parties?" *American Journal of Political Science* 29 (February 1985): 139–60.

Harris, Frederick, and Linda Williams. "JCPS/Gallup Poll Reflects Changing Views on Political Issues," *Focus* 14 (1986): 3–6.

Hershey, Marjorie R. "The Politics of Androgyny: Sex Roles and Attitudes toward Women in Politics," *American Politics Quarterly* 5 (July 1977): 216–37.

Hibbing, John R. "Hispanic Representation in the U.S. Congress." In Rodolfo O. De la Garza, et al., eds. *The Mexican-American Experience: An Interdisciplinary Approach.* Austin: University of Texas Press, 1985, pp. 259–66.

Hill, Samuel L. "Religion and Region in America," *The Annals* 480 (July 1985): 132–41.

Howe, Maxine. "Latin Politicians Focus on Registration Effort," *New York Times,* Section B, March 30, 1984, p. 1.

Kincaid, Dianne, and Ann R. Henry. "The Family Factor in State Legislative Turnover," *Legislative Studies Quarterly* 6 (March 1981): 55–68.

Kraus, Wilma Rule. "Political Implications of Gender Roles: A Review of the Literature," *American Political Science Review* 68 (December 1974): 1706–23.

Lehman, Nicholas. "The Origins of the Underclass," *The Atlantic Monthly,* June 1986, pp. 31–55.

Lewis, I. A., and William Schneider. "Black Voting, Bloc Voting, and the Democrats," *Public Women* 6 (1983): 12–15.

Lewis-Beck, Michael S. "Election Forecasts in 1984: How Accurate Are They?" *PS* 19 (Winter 1985): 53–62.

Lewis-Beck, Michael S., and Tom W. Rice. "Forecasting U.S. House Elections," *Legislative Studies Quarterly* 9 (November 1984): 475–86.

"Los Angeles Comes of Age," *The Economist,* April 3, 1982, p. 12.

Merritt, Shayne. "Sex Roles and Political Ambition," *Sex Roles* 8 (September 1982): 1035.

Mezey, Susan Gluck. "Does Sex Make a Difference?" *Western Political Quarterly* 31 (December 1978): 492–501.

Miller, Warren E., and Donald E. Stokes. "Constituency Influence in Congress," *American Political Science Review* 57 (March 1973): 45–56.

More, Ronnie, and Marvin Rich. "When Blacks Take Office," *The Progressive* 3 (May 1972): 31.

Nechemias, Carol. "Geographic Mobility and Women's Access to State Legislatures," *Western Political Quarterly* 38 (March 1985): 119–31.

Nelson, Albert J. "Political Culture and Women's Representation in Lower State Legislative Chambers," *International Journal of Intercultural Relations* 4 (1980): 367–77.

____. "Women's Advancement as Chairpersons: 1979 and 1983," *International Journal of Intercultural Relations* 4 (1987): 401–10.

____. "Women's Potential Influence in Lower State Legislative Chambers, 1985 to 1986," *Wisconsin Political Scientist* 2 (Fall 1987): 13–19.

New York Times. February 16, 1986, p. 27a.

Niemi, Richard G., and Laura Winsky. "Membership Turnover in the U.S. State Legislatures," *Legislative Studies Quarterly* 12 (February 1987): 115–24.

Peek, Charles W., and Sharon Brown. "Sex Prejudice among White Protestants: Like or Unlike Ethnic Prejudice," *Social Forces* 59 (September 1980): 169–85.

Polsby, Nelson W. "The Institutionalization of the U.S. House of Representatives," *American Political Science Review* 63 (March 1968): 787–807.

Powell, Brian, and Lola Carr Steelman. "Fundamentalism and Sexism: A Reanalysis of Peek and Brown," *Social Forces* 60 (June 1982): 1154–67.

Ranney, Austin. "Parties in State Politics." In Herbert Jacob and Kenneth N. Vines, eds., *Politics in the American States.* Boston: Little, Brown, 1976, pp. 51–92.

Ray, David. "The Source of Voting Cues in Three State Legislatures," *Journal of Politics* 44 (1982): 1074–87.

Rhodes, A. Lewis. "Effects of Religious Denominations in Occupational Choices," *Sex Roles* 9 (January 1983): 93–108.

Rosenthal, Alan. "Turnover in State Legislatures," *American Journal of Political Science* 18 (1974): 606–16.

Rule, Wilma. "Why Women Don't Run," *Western Political Quarterly* 34 (March 1984): 60–77.

San Miguel, Guadalupe. "Conflict and Controversy in the Evolution of Bilingual Education in the United States — An Interpretation." In Rodolfo O. De la Garza, et al., eds., *The Mexican-American Experience: An Interdisciplinary Approach.* Austin: University of Texas Press, 1985.

Shapiro, Robert Y., and Mahajan Harprett. "Gender Differences in Policy Preferences: A Summary of Trends from the 1960s to the 1980s," *Public Opinion Quarterly* 50 (1986): 42–61.

Shinn, Kwang S., and John S. Jackson III. "Membership Turnover in U.S. State Legislatures, 1931–1976," *Legislative Studies Quarterly* 4 (February 1979): 95–104.

Shortridge, James R. "A Regionalization of American Religion," *Journal for the Scientific Study of Religion* 16 (June 1977): 143–54.

Squire, Peverill. "Career Opportunities and Membership Stability in Legislatures," *Legislative Studies Quarterly* 13 (February 1988): 65–77.

Stoper, Emily. "Wife and Politician: Role Strain among Women in Public Office." In Marianne Githens and Jewell S. Prestage, eds., *A Portrait of Marginality.* New York: David McKay, 1977.

Tobin, James. "Reaganomics in Retrospect." In B. B. Kymlicka and Jean V. Matthews, eds., *The Reagan Revolution?* Chicago: Dorsey Press, 1988, pp. 85–103.

Uslaner, Eric M., and Ronald E. Weber. "U.S. State Legislators' Opinions of Constituency Attitudes," *Legislative Studies Quarterly* 4 (November 1979): 536–86.

Weisberg, Robert. "Assessing Legislator-Constituency Policy Agreement," *Legislative Studies Quarterly* 4 (November 1979): 605–22.

Welch, Susan. "Are Women More Liberal Than Men in the U.S. Congress?" *Legislative Studies Quarterly* 10 (February 1985): 125–34.

____. "Recruitment of Women to Public Office: A Discriminant Analysis," *Western Political Quarterly* 31 (September 1978): 372–80.

Welch, Susan, and John R. Hibbing. "Hispanic Representation in the U.S. Congress." In Rodolfo O. De la Garza, et al., eds., *The Mexican-American Experience: An Interdisciplinary Approach.* Austin: University of Texas Press, 1985, pp. 259–66.

Witt, Elder. "Are Our Governments Paying What It Takes to Keep the Best and the Brightest?" *Governing* 2 (December 1988): 30–39.

Wilcox, Clyde, and Elizabeth Adell Cook. "Evangelical Women and Feminism," *Women and Politics* 9 (1981): 27–49.

Wollenberg, Ernest. "Correlates of the Equal Rights Amendment," *Social Science Quarterly* 60 (March 1980): 676–84.

Zelinsky, Wilbur. "An Approach to Religious Geography in the United States," *Annals of the Association of American Geographers* 51 (June 1981).

UNPUBLISHED MANUSCRIPTS

De Stafano, Christine. "Postmodernism/Postfeminism." Paper presented at the 1987 Annual Meeting of the American Political Science Association, Chicago, Illinois.

Francis, Wayne L. "Agenda Setting and the Potential for Reciprocity in Legislatures." Paper presented at the 1986 Annual Meeting of the Midwest Political Science Association, Chicago, Illinois.

Hamm, Keith E., and Ronald D. Hedlund. "Occupational Interests and State Legislative Committees." Paper presented at the 1989 Annual Meeting of the Midwest Political Science Association, Chicago, Illinois.

Hedlund, Ronald D., and Dianne Powers. "Constancy of Committee Membership in 16 States: 1971–1986." Paper presented at the 1987 Annual Meeting of the Midwest Political Science Association, Chicago, Illinois.

Kahn, Kim Frederick, and Edie N. Goldenburg. "Evaluations of Male and Female U.S. Senate Candidates." Paper presented at the 1988 Annual Meeting of the Midwest Political Science Association, Chicago, Illinois.

Nelson, Albert J. "Decline of Elazar's Cultural Concept in Explaining Women's Representation." Unpublished paper at the University of Wisconsin-LaCrosse, LaCrosse, Wisconsin, 1988.

____. "Representation and Turnover of Women, Blacks, and Hispanics in Eight States." Paper presented at the 1989 Annual Meeting of the Midwest Political Science Association, Chicago, Illinois.

____. "Women's Political Influence in Lower State Legislative Chambers." Paper presented at the 1987 Annual Meeting of the Midwest Political Science Association, Chicago, Illinois.

Peterson, Steven A. "Church Participation and Political Participation: The Spillover Effect." Paper presented at the 1990 Annual Meeting of the Midwest Political Science Association, Chicago, Illinois.

Petrocik, John R. "Issues and Agendas: Electoral Coalitions in the 1988 Election." Paper presented at the 1989 Annual Meeting of the Midwest Political Science Association, Chicago, Illinois.

Thomas, Sue. "The Impact of Women on State Legislative Policies." Paper presented at the 1989 Annual Meeting of the Midwest Political Science Association, Atlanta, Georgia.

Thomas, Sue, and Susan Welch. "The Impact of Gender on Activities and Priorities of State Legislators." Paper presented at the 1989 Annual Meeting of the Midwest Political Science Association, Chicago, Illinois.

Shinn, Kwang Shik. *Innovation Adoption and Diffusion in the Political System of States: A Focus on Taxation and Antidiscrimination.* Carbondale: Ph.D. dissertation at Southern Illinois University, 1979.

Van der Slik, Jack R. "Legislative Performance: Comparing Aspirations, Styles, and Achievement of Women and Men Members of the Illinois General Assembly." Paper presented at the 1988 Annual Meeting of the Midwest Political Science Association, Chicago, Illinois.

Wilcox, Clyde. "Lingering Support for the Christian Right: Robertson and the Christian Right Groups in 1988." Paper presented at the 1990 Annual Meeting of the Midwest Political Science Association, Chicago, Illinois.

Yoder, Brad. "Social Welfare in the United States before 1914." Presentation at the National Endowment for the Humanities Summer Seminar on the American Regulatory and Welfare State, Nashville, Vanderbilt University, 1988.

SUBJECT INDEX

AUTHOR INDEX

ABOUT THE AUTHOR

ALBERT J. NELSON is Assistant Professor of Political Science at the University of Wisconsin–LaCrosse. His publications include journal articles and contributed chapters on women and minorities in state legislatures and a variety of other political issues.

ABOUT THE AUTHOR